After Life, What?

A Post-Death Quest

Robert Pinansky

THE BOOK TREE
San Diego, California

Originally published 1995
The Book Tree
San Diego

© 1995 Robert Pinansky
© 2004 Nick Pinansky
All rights reserved

ISBN 1-58509-121-9

Published by
The Book Tree
P O Box 16476
San Diego, CA 92176
www.thebooktree.com

We provide fascinating and educational products to help awaken the public to new ideas and information that would not be available otherwise
Call 1 (800) 700-8733 for our *FREE BOOK TREE CATALOG*

TO NATALIE

Who gave of herself for 38 years and whom I dearly miss.

Love in your heart wasn't put there to stay
Love isn't love till you give it away.

CONTENTS

1. I Met God	7
2. Seven Months Later	13
3. One Year Later	15
4. Science And Philosophy	19
5. Philosophy and Parapsychology	29
6. Psychokinesis	33
7. Personal Experiences	37
8. Related ESP Phenomena	41
9. Personal Thoughts and Quotes	47
10. Reincarnation	57
11. Out-of-Body Experiences and Memory	71
12. Death is the Gate of Life	79
13 Thoughts on Religion	85
14. Raison D'Etre	95
Epilogue	99
Suggested Readings	101

INTRODUCTION

My grandfather, Robert Pinansky, was leading an average middle-class suburban life. One day in 1977, while engaged in the mundane task of mowing the lawn, his world, as he knew it was suddenly and profoundly altered. He suffered, as the doctors termed it, a fatal heart attack. Pronounced clinically dead, but subsequently resuscitated, he had a near-death experience (NDE). The event was so powerful that following his miraculous recovery he embarked upon a personal quest. This "quest for truth" lasted for over twenty years. His quest for knowledge and understanding of what happened to him became an avocation of research into experiences of existence after death and the substance and very meaning of life itself.

During his recollections and reflections on his own near-death experience he came to the realization that God, as he understood, had shown him what, or who, was of true importance in his life and allowed him to return to life with a purpose or a mission. The mission that became apparent to my grandfather was to help and comfort others by attempting to alleviate their fears of death with enlightenment. It was to communicate to others the truth of what lay beyond this material life and to have faith in the presence of a supreme and loving power.

Robert Pinansky was a gregarious and determined man. He eventually shared his experiences and spread his message widely by lecturing at universities and being a guest speaker on various radio and television talk shows. Among his credits are lecturing at Western New Mexico University, the Phoenix Nights television show, and the "700 Club". He worked with other researchers such as Dr. Kenneth Ring and the International Association for Near Death Study (IANDS).

Contained in this book are portions of his explorations and ponderings formulated during his quest for knowledge of various world religions, natural and physical sciences, philosophy, and meta-physics. Originally, the book was titled the Latin, <u>Quo Veritas? - A Post Death Quest</u>, meaning, "what is the truth?" To this end, my grandfather kept his mind open to all old and new ideas and information. He kept his faith in a loving and all-knowing God strong. And he listened with interest and compassion to other people's stories of otherworldly experiences, including my own which is briefly told within this book. He abandoned all preconceived ideas on religion, life, and death that he had held from earlier in his life or had formed while growing up. He completely opened himself up to new ways of thinking and believing.

Although my grandfather has made his final journey to the light, I hope by continuing to publish this book, my grandfather's mission is accomplished. I feel that I am fortunate to have such a valuable legacy of knowledge and love to share with you.

Nicholas Robert Pinansky

PREFACE

On April 18, 1977, I underwent a wondrous experience which changed my entire outlook on life. This mystical, ecclesiastic event was a true, spiritual, out-of-body happening.

After a full life of ordinary living, an accepting and non-questioning life, I was projected into a medium of thought alien to anything I had ever known before. The veil of death had a rent, through which a ray of light had touched me.

Unanswerable questions ran rampant through my mind. Were there any answers that I could understand? My quest began then, and it still continues. I hope it will open the door for others.

I have read exhaustively and tried to include in this book information to help the ordinary reader realize how much evidence of life beyond our present realm exists. No responsibility is assumed for errors, inaccuracies, omissions, or any inconsistencies herein. This book is of my own thoughts and experiences and is in no way intended to represent any psychic, mental, spiritual, or ecclesiastical mores of the present day.

The following is a true experience of what happened to me and is written to the best of my ability.

FOREWORD

In writing of my experience, I wonder who will read it. What will be the effect of this experience on the reader? If I can alleviate or diminish the fear of death or of the hereafter, for anyone at all, I will feel that I have accomplished my goal.

Most professional scientists communicate in words or phrases incomprehensible to the average person. Like a doctor stating that you are suffering from "a contusion and abrasion at the proximal end of the distal phalanx, posterior surface," when you hit the end of your finger with a hammer. Instead of simplifying, they complicate and entangle situations, using scientific words or phrases of Latin. Perhaps this keeps us from questioning their financial tabulations. What I attempt to do is state in simple language what experts like to explain in complex technical terms.

Years back, when I was in business, I didn't have any special interest in "weirdo" philosophies; my interest in religion was low and I was much too busy to spend any time meditating over the more profound aspects of life and death. Twilight-type tales were interesting reading, but what did they have to do with me?
One morning all this changed. I died, and I returned. The experience stunned me; I was in shock for a long time. I may have looked and sounded the same as before, but mentally I was not the same person.

I kept asking "Why me?" Never, to my knowledge, had I done anything to deserve this wondrous, mystical unveiling, to experience the feeling of universal love towards humanity. The fear of death and the future was replaced by a longing to return to what we call God, since there are no human words to define and explain the experience fully.

After a few months of recuperation, my quest began. After six months of reading and studying, I thought that I was quite knowledgeable. After a few years of studying, I realized how little I knew. Now, after intensive studying and research, I know how very much knowledge I lack, but I have at least opened the door a small crack.

As time went on I left my "high" and returned to the "norm" of everyday living. I like to think that I have become a better person and only wish that I could have sustained the mental keenness and awareness that I possessed for quite a while, right after the near-death experience.

This is a very personal story. I do not wish to get involved in theology or any abstract theories about God. I am simply trying to relate some of what I have learned during the past years. I have no argument with any of the scientists in these fields who, I am sure, know more than I. I wish to relate to the average person without being clever or confusing.

To examine and question that which we have been taught to be true all our lives is difficult. To deny a lifetime of self-evident thoughts is mind boggling and hard to accept. Suddenly, a straight line is a curve and one plus one no longer equals two. I try to simplify concepts that are hard to grasp without being a philosopher.

When we try to explain things that stretch the human imagination to its utmost, we must know the basic facts of extraordinary phenomena. It is hard to explain something that requires quantum physics to those whose limit is long division.

Intelligence gives us the power to analyze things in a proper perspective. Knowledge enables us to understand what is spiritual and what is material.

It is necessary to study to know, to know to understand, to understand to judge. All I wish to do is to open the door. To enter this room of knowledge you must go past me and find the answers for yourself.

My philosophies and thoughts are intermingled in my writing and, of course, are influenced by my readings. I sincerely hope that in seeking your own answers, you find my thoughts a help.

Chapter One

I MET GOD

Before my experience, if anyone had made the above statement to me, I would have classified them with the flying saucer believers or religious fanatics. I have experienced such an amazing, wonderful, beautiful time that I feel the story should be told, in the hope that it will wipe away the fear of death and the unknown that is so pervasive.

On April 18, 1977, at about 11:30 A.M., I died and was later returned to life. After reading this statement, I fully realize the thoughts that most people will have – but please bear with me.

For months after this happened, I have been saying to myself, "Why me?" Why was I singled out, out of millions, to be given this glorious knowledge? I don't think I will ever know – but since then I have discovered that I am not alone in this experience. I recently read a little on the subject and was astounded to discover how many others had experienced almost exactly the same thing.

Ridicule and not being believed is hard to accept when you are only trying to enrich other's lives by sharing your experiences with them. Quiet and forbearance becomes the rule when sometimes you feel like shouting from the steeples a message of love and hope to all mankind. I can find no human words to express emotions involved in much that I am trying to relate.

On the morning of my experience, I was raking leaves in front of my house on a beautiful spring day, when I suddenly knew something was wrong. Dizziness and a partial loss of vision alarmed me, and I made my way into the house. I was afraid at the time that I was having a stroke. Luckily, my wife was home and she phoned the police. An excruciating pain radiated across my chest. I remember being placed in a litter, and the pain became unbearable. I was slipping in and out of consciousness, and then went into a completely unconscious state and knew nothing of what was happening around me. I was later told that I was rushed into the hospital emergency room, and they started working on me.

Suddenly, I was in an ethereal state above the room, looking down ("looking" is not the correct word, but it is as close as I can come). I saw and was cognizant of everything. One doctor, whom I could describe vividly, said, "He is gone." The other said what sounded like, "Let's try so many watt seconds." They had a paddle under me and on my chest. I saw the room and these people whom I had never seen before, around my body while I was in this detached state. I was not in a human physical shape, but more ethereal, cellular, cloudlike.

I left the area and travelled upward through a sea of darkness studded with pin points of distant lights similar to stars, until the most beautiful, warm, golden, radiant arch surrounded me. Below this, under a cloud-like floor, was a series of parallel, grey, upright cylindrical torpedo-like shapes, appearing almost like shrouded, hooded monks going off into the distance, which at the same time I did not understand.

A brilliant, white/yellow, warm pillar of light confronted me. The light was a brilliant, blinding effulgence, fiery and immeasurable as the sun. I was now in a light golden, cellular embodiment.

The light radiated warmth, compassion, and wisdom. It expanded awareness. It flooded my mind. Everything was comprehended instantly. Part of the general message: learn to love people and acquire knowledge.

The light, this is a force of pure intelligence. It is total energy consisting of pure love and all the elements in the world. It is a constructive force that cannot be analyzed. Part of this is in everyone.

The greatest feelings of warmth, love, and tenderness became part of me. My consciousness or soul was at the foot or base. When I tried to look up (not exactly so, but the closest words I can use), I saw the sweet smile and love of my father at the time when I was a young child, and he held me and loved me. I felt this love permeating my being (I had never had any conscious remembrance of his love, nor had I thought of my father for years). Instantly a scroll of my life was laid bare and open to this wonderful presence, "GOD". I felt inside my being his forgiveness for the things in my life I was ashamed of, as though they were not of great importance.

I was asked – but there were no words – one question. It was a straight, mental, instantaneous communication: *What had I done to benefit or advance the human race?* At the same time, my entire life was presented instantly in front of me and I was shown, or made to understand, what counted. I will not go into this further except to say that what I had considered *un*important in life was my salvation, and what I thought was important was nil, nothing.

I was made to understand that we were put on earth for God's purpose, and anyone who destroys another human being is working at cross purposes to God's will. This also applies to self destruction or suicide. All of this was communicated instantly to me, with no time element as we know it.

There was an infinite sea of golden cells below as part of this blinding presence in which I was about to become assimilated. Suddenly, I was withdrawn and became an elongated, cellular presence just outside of the golden-orange arch. I was now given the choice of going either way. The mental torment I experienced (no physical pain) is indescribable. I felt something like a worm when it is impaled on a fish hook, and writhes and twists violently, fighting for release. I wrestled and twisted and turned, inside a cellular state.

It is impossible to describe such mental agony.

What influenced me to return was the fact that I hadn't said "good-bye" to my wife, or had time to tell her how thankful I was for her love and devotion, and how I felt about her and my children. So many things were also left undone. What would she do about them without me? So I returned to my body and into an unconscious state. I knew nothing more until I woke in an intensive care unit with a nurse holding my hand telling me not to be afraid; that they would take good care of me.

I have tried to retell this experience just as it was, but there are no words to interpret some of the happenings and feelings.

After my release from the hospital, I found that certain senses to which I had once paid no attention were more alert and sharp. For example, the sky was more blue, a tree and its leaves were more green, everything was so very beautiful. I could almost smell and taste the air and wind. I became cognizant of things which I had previously taken for granted. And I felt a tremendous love for all humanity.

I also had a longing or desire to return to that wonderful place – not exactly a death wish, but a feeling that I had missed something. This is diminishing with the passing of time. I also have a feeling I can't describe or put into words... that something within me, or my brain, or whatever, is missing. I can't seem to think the way I did previously; a certain power of recall seems missing.

I have tried to analyze this entire occurrence in relation to dreams, semi-conscious thought, or hallucinations. There is absolutely no comparison. About five months later I went back into the hospital to see if the emergency room was the same as I had seen it in an unconscious state. There it was, the open doorway, the cabinet, the walls. I had never been in this room before, consciously, yet recognized it. I have no further explanation.

Perhaps you are wondering about me. Why am I telling this? Is he a mental case or some kind of nut? Previous to my experience, I would have felt the same way. I am just an average person – 59 years old when this occurred, and never a very religious person.

Before my experience, when I visited or entered any holy house of worship, temples, churches, and shrines included, I often felt an inner sense of spiritual holiness, an indescribable feeling of awe and mental awareness. One time, years ago, when I approached the shrine at St. Anne De Beaupre, Quebec, my skin and hair tingled as though I was in an electrical field. I have a similar feeling when I look upon the beauty and wonder of nature, which I love. The sunset on a prairie, a lake in the wilderness in the early morn, a mountain range in the distance, anything of this nature stirs my soul. This has intensified since my experience.

Since teen-aged years I have experienced, on rare occasions, a brilliancy similar to what I experienced in a disembodied state. This has occurred a few times while in a semi-conscious state before passing into a deep sleep. I seem to see a long funnel-like tunnel and at the end I get a glimpse of a super-strong light of great brilliancy, at times, as I get closer. Several times this nova has seemed to flash or explode in my brain with a sharp intensity. The brilliancy was somewhat similar to the one I saw while disembodied. I am not able to explain this.

Chapter Two

SEVEN MONTHS LATER

17 July 1978.

Since I wrote of the events that occurred at the time of my earthly demise due to my heart attack, I have given much thought and study to this psychic experience. I thought mine was unique; I know now that hundreds of others have experienced similar phenomena. More and more people are becoming interested and believers in the immortality of their psychic being, soul, or whatever you want to call the part of God that is within you.

I asked every doctor I met if he had any experience with patients who had had an "out-of-body experience" and received negative answers until I was finally referred to Dr. Moody's book, *Life After Life*. Months after I wrote of my experience I read the book and was stunned. Entire excerpts by other people researched were almost as if I had written them. The similarity is far beyond the realm of coincidence. Moody's sequel, *Reflections on Life After Life*, clarified certain things I had seen which I hadn't written about, since I wasn't clear about their meaning.
I now became very interested in psychic phenomena, or the realm of the unknown, and have been looking for the answer to "What is the present existence?" Most studies have been those which have been scientifically documented by parapsychology professors or other authors who are not writing for sensationalism. The immensity of the field and the amount of research amazed me. I have read of documented occurrences that I once would have scoffed at, as do most

people today, without a fair investigation.

Mediums, spiritualism, psychic phenomena, psychics, sensitives, automatic writing, out-of-body experiences, survivals: these are a few of the subjects in the entire parapsychological field that I have been delving into. We all must seek for ourselves knowledge that is of interest and meaning to us.

A beautiful quote by a psychic impressed me. "You always were and always will be. This is the meaning of existence and joy. The God that is, is within you, for you are a part of all that is."

I can't state all of my present thoughts and beliefs, because my search has just begun; but part of what I believe to be the ultimate answer is that a personal understanding has to be attained by each of us. We must do everything we can to become knowledgeable.

There is a rhythm of appearing and disappearing. In all of nature there is no end without a beginning of something new. Man's task is development, whether it takes 30 years or 30,000 years. Time is only relative. The goal is to become a perfect human being before we can rise to a new realm. Dying is only a change to another polarity. Birth and death are very similar; every ending is also a beginning.

People seem to have a dread of the unknown that is eradicated with understanding. I don't believe we will ever know all the answers, nor were we meant to know all, but knowledge makes our present life more beautiful. The more I know, the more I know how little I know.

I have been enjoying life with a greater mental intensity than I did previous to my experience, but as time passes the vividity is lessening. With the increasing normalcy of life, I am being blunted by the forces of everyday living. Thankfulness and contemplation have lessened as I advance. The small things of joy and beauty I am taking more for granted than I did a year ago. Physical living is contesting the ethereal part. The flame of love for humanity is not burning as brightly as it was a year ago. Is death the catalyst that creates love and life? I wonder, I truly wonder.

Chapter Three

ONE YEAR LATER

June, 1979.

It is now over two years since my heart attack and extra-sensory, "out-of-body" experience (OBE). Since that time, I have been seeking knowledge of what transpires at death and after. A vast amount of literature by many people who are delving and seeking knowledge and truth in many countries has been written. Voluminous reading has helped me to recognize what books and authors have value. Some are sensationalists or are misguided (most of them honestly), having been unduly influenced by their own experiences. You have to relate yourself to the rest of the world's knowledge and say, "Thank you, God," for having felt the love and insight that you should be entitled to only once as a mortal.

There are so many reports of the death experience that everyone, scientists or not, must bow to the convincing evidence. All seem to follow the same general pattern of experiences, with small variances. There is an affinity felt when two experiencers meet, and many times there is an emotional flow of love between them.

Many religions are practiced by the people of this earth. The religions of most people are not a matter of choice, but of birth. They follow their parental teachings. They tend to reject, without knowledge or evaluation, that which differs. Small physiological differences in mankind have been part of the cause of their harassment of each other. We must respect all human beings. Even a lifetime religious scholar would learn only a smattering of all there is to know. I've concluded that most paths ultimately lead to the same altar; they all reach for a Supreme Being of Love.

Reports by people who have experienced death and returned say they see someone they love, be it a deity they worshipped or a mortal, to help them transfer over. Philosophers, through logic, reach this same level. They all arrive at the door to heaven.

Today, there is much documented and scientifically presented evidence on the Near Death Experience (NDE). Do we press on and go further? What then? Christian philosophers shy away, feeling that this is an occult or forbidden religion. Most religions give no definite explanations or promises. The only ones who enter this realm are the mystics or psychics. The similarity of their descriptions of a spiritual life, with no collaboration among them, is amazing. They all describe various levels or planes in which there are "Halls of Knowledge" which must be attended before attaining higher levels. "In my Father's house are many mansions." Higher planes are reached as the spiritual capacity is extended. Ultimately the highest joy is attained.

Some think the cycle is then begun again, with a new physical return as the spiritual essence or energy wears down, the same as in a corporeal body. Others differ. Most agree that what we sow in one life, we will reap in a latter – the theory of karma. The spiritual survival hypothesis is agreed upon by most people who have read any of the copious material written on this subject. Sharing self both mentally and physically enlarges the spirit.

Spiritualistic existence is hard to discuss with the average person who either has a slightly morbid curiosity or will completely reject any hypothesis. Regardless of evidence, the will to disbelieve is far greater than the will to believe. We cannot delve into this realm and attempt to rationalize evidence, using only our limited senses. In our everyday realm our language is adequate for description, but in the realm of mental experiences such as the near-death experience, there is no language that is relevant to the data received.

The language of written material is very difficult for the layman to understand due to its pedantic style, statistical coldness, and unbelievability in its attempt to entertain. The non-physical nature of the many demonstrations of psychic phenomena baffles researchers and scientists.

Many opinions are expressed about paranormal phenomena, both pro and con, by people who are ignorant of the large amount of psychic research done in this field. The spiritual is composed of a different type of time and matter, as opposed to our physical realm. There is a power above and beyond human nature whose motivating force is Love.

In my post-mortem life everything has become more precious. Beauty is intensified. Even the simple things of life become more precious when the fear of death is non-existent.

No life experience can help you understand a mystical experience. It is not different in degree; it is a different *kind* of experience. It is not understandable until you experience it yourself. All knowledge is interwoven; everything is seen in the light of everything else. All is coalesced and related. All is one, merging into the cosmos of God.

I shall continue to seek knowledge as long as I am able to, but know that soon the answer will be revealed. From a medical viewpoint, I know time is getting short. I consider myself fortunate to have been "touched by God" and to have had trepidation replaced by expectancy and love.

Chapter Four

SCIENCE AND PHILOSOPHY

My studies have strengthened the belief that began with my out-of-body experience, the belief that life as we know it is one small part of our existence in a cosmos that is made up of innumerable plateaus not visible to our present senses. Every once in a while we receive a message from a level other than our own. Before my near-death miracle, I disregarded such signs, passing them off as odd, freakish, or even fraudulent. Much of the following material I have gathered so that you may share with me the many signs we have been given to allow us to strengthen our faith in an existence beyond our present one, an existence we can understand only slightly but which may become clearer to us as we study, research, and watch for its manifestation.

The words and teachings of all the great prophets of divinity have been twisted by mankind over the years so I wonder if what I have to say will make any difference. My life has been unexceptional but for the fact that I was permitted to see for a short time through a curtain of death. Since my return I have been constantly seeking the answer to what life is about.

Since man has been able to think, he has striven for the answer to this puzzle. I only hope that my thoughts may add a little to those who are also seeking the truth of the soul.

Some believe that science is the only study that can rationalize and understand the world. Nothing else is real. Others believe science is only one of the many ways to comprehend the world. Human thought has many different modes.

Scientific investigation is now being extended into territory which was the realm of only mystics and psychics. Scientists are now trying to find the golden path to heaven.

There are two kinds of doubt. One says "this is completely impossible." Discussions and rationalization are wasted against this attitude. The second doubt is more open, saying "it may be improbable but if any truth is there, you must take the time and effort to look, listen, and research."

All our lives we are taught certain facts that seem logical, so we accept them without question. It is hard to have to disregard much that we have been taught by those we have always considered more intelligent and more knowledgeable than ourselves. Let us look back just a few hundred years.

The scientists and teachers of that time told us that the earth was the center of the universe and that the sun revolved around it. Why, anyone could see it rises in the east and sets in the west. How foolish are you? The earth rotating through space at a thousand miles per hour? We would all go flying off! Yet now, we accept our place in the universe without question. How many could figure this for themselves without being taught?

Knowledge left to us by the great thinkers of the past is like the light of the stars that still reaches us even though those stars disappeared years ago.

Look at the beautiful stars tonight. Tomorrow in daylight they are invisible, but when I say they are still there – even though you can't see them – you don't question me. Why? Because someone else also said so? Ever try to figure it out for yourself?

We are so accustomed to trusting our physical senses that when they are taken away, we are frightened. I see it, I can touch it, taste it, smell it, hear it; therefore it is. How else can we judge?

I remember when I was in Disneyland and saw "ghosts" in the Haunted House. Of course I know they were only projected holographic light forms: someone had to explain it to me. But what if it were someplace else and not explained? I saw it with my own eyes but how many would believe me?

In a museum of science is a coin in a saucer that is seen in three solid dimensions. When you try to pick it up, your finger passes right through it. It is another projection that you can see and yet isn't there. A miracle? No, just science at work – but what if you saw it someplace else without any explanation? I wonder what you would think.

The science and technologies of advanced intelligences appear as magic to us when they violate our laws of physics, simply because we do not understand. What we see is largely what we have been taught by our culture. We have been taught to organize our perceptions. We assume "facts" that are not always true. Look at a tree. You endow it with a hardness and interior under the bark even though you don't see it. You take for granted that it will still be there when you look away and then back. You endow it with a permanence. You go beyond the strict data provided by your senses. Our perceptions are distorted due to the limitations of our sense organs, which can receive only a small amount of the phenomena of the universe.

Using your eyes is using an imperfect sense to make a judgement. Without light in a dark room what can you see? Can you see the nearest thing – your eyelid? Can you see the distant stars in the daylight? Your other senses such as touch, taste, and smell are also limited. The mind is imperfect. If you base your thoughts on limited and imperfect sensory perceptions, how can you have perfect conclusions?

In advanced physics a straight line can be a curved line when a gravitational force curves space. When we deal with speeds approaching that of light, mass and energy become interrelated, $E=MC^2$. In the same way when we try to find answers in a metaphysical field, we have to realize that our everyday senses are not enough. The knowledge we use to examine a premise sometimes is not sufficient. We cannot explain parallel lines meeting in Euclid geometry. We cannot explain events forbidden by a system within that system.

Our ability to comprehend is limited by our lack of knowledge. In the near future, the study of man's immortality will be commonly accepted as a basic science and not thought of as "way out."

We try to explain everything from a physical matter point of view, from the atom to the universe. How do we explain that which has no matter, such as love or thought? No one will deny their existence, yet try to prove them by physical scientific laws.

I once had a very smart dog. He would sit for hours and watch television with me. Yet if I had tried to explain to him how these wavelengths are broadcast over the ether, he would never understand. Maybe our brains, at the present evolutionary stage of development, can only comprehend so much.

To an insect on a leaf the plant is the entire universe. What can he know of the vast oceans and continents that exist? What if we were in the same position to the cosmos as this bug is to the world? What makes us so important? The answers to these questions are part of what I have been seeking.

Pot Shots

We see only a small amount of the visual spectrum. What we actually see is limited by our eyesight. The range of visible light waves, compared to what exists, is a very tiny portion compared to the whole. We know the others exist. They go from cosmic on up through radio waves. What if we could see them?

WAVELENGTHS (Cms.)

$10^{\frac{14}{}}$ $10^{\frac{9}{}}$

Unknown
Cosmic Rays
Gamma Rays
X-Ray
Ultraviolet
Visible Light
Infra Red
Heat Waves
Electrical Discharge
Radar
Television
Short Radio
Broadcast
Long Radio
Unknown

Two people can see the same thing at the same time and yet see two different things. For example: If I shoot an arrow from a bow to a target directly across the room, everyone in the room would say it travelled in a straight line. But what if I were to stand outside the room – enclose the room so that no one could see out and have the target aligned straight to me from outside of the room. Supposing this were in space and I moved the building or room upwards just as the arrow was loosed. It would then enter at the top left wall and go out the bottom right, while moving straight towards the target. Anyone in the room would say it travelled in a diagonal direction, while anyone outside would say it went straight. Who is right? They both are. We cannot always believe what we see.

We can not always believe what we see.

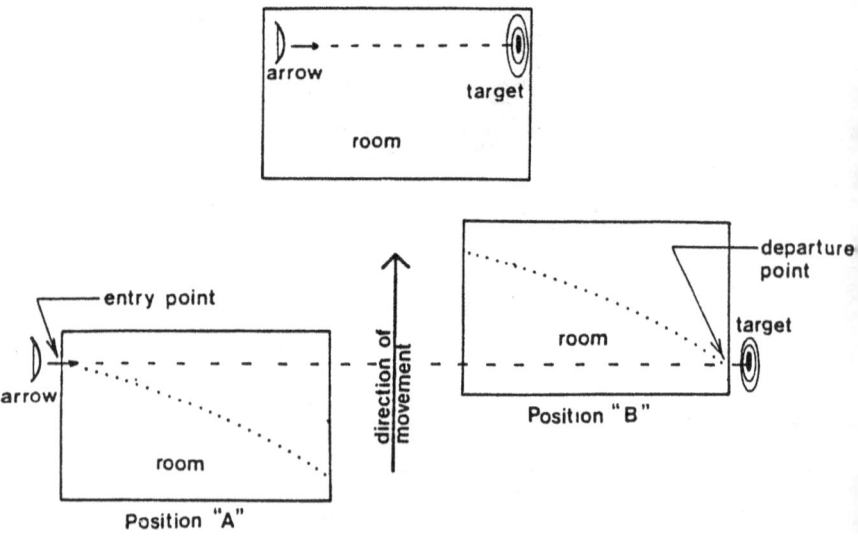

Fig. 1

Another example, as explained by Dr. Einstein: Imagine two people standing face to face next to a railroad track. In the distance, left and right, two bolts of lightning strike simultaneously. Both people see both bolts at the same time.

Now put one of these people on a train approaching the other, who is standing still. At the time they arrive directly opposite from each other, the two bolts of lightning strike simultaneously again. Will they both see the bolts at the same time? No, the person on the train will see the bolt he is moving away from after the person who is standing still. In fact, if the train moves theoretically at the speed of light, he will never see one of the lightning bolts.

Here it is, two people at the same place at the same time and they do not see the same thing. This is Einstein's philosophy, the Relativity of Simultaneity. Man cannot assume that his sense of "now" applies to all parts of the universe. The following statement by Einstein is often quoted: "The most beautiful and profound emotion we can experience is the sense of the mystical. It is the source of all true science."

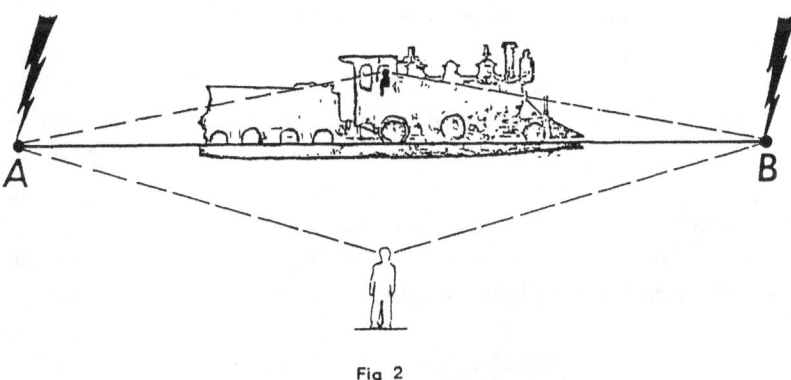

Fig 2

The strongest emotion is love. Not physical love, but the all-encompassing love of humanity, the universe, and all therein. Our society and social upbringing sublimate this. We teach it and say "listen and live by the words of all the great prophets." Yet what is it within most of us that denies this?

We are afraid of anything strange and different, but do not take the time or make the effort to investigate that difference. In the name of religion, how many millions have been exterminated? Yet do not all religions fundamentally preach the same thing? "Do unto others as you would have them do unto you," and "Thou shalt not kill." It may be said in strange tongues and different ways, but all are striving to reach the same answer.

How many of us have ever taken the time to learn what others believe? We deny without reason, while we believe as we do only because of birth. Our parents were such and so, therefore so are we.

Remember – but for an accident of birth you might be in your enemy's shoes. Tolerance? We destroy and kill without rhyme or reason. We all have prejudices, be they against color, race, or something else strange. Different social amenities and customs we ridicule and disparage because we do not understand. It is easier to ridicule than to investigate. We follow our parents and peers; we "swim with the tide." If we question, we ourselves may be thought of as strange. Thank God for the few who are not afraid to march out of step; they push the rest of the world forward.

I have friends whom I have known all my life – good people, judged from our present moral and social positions, yet the discussion of religious prejudices disturbs them. Respectable bigotry prevails in most societies. This is the way they were raised and taught. They are satisfied, and do not want any "waves."

To seek God and the truth of existence, we have to question and sift; even when we think we know something, we must question it.

There is so much more ultimately coming than this transient illusion called mortal life. A future is coming, but not easily, wherein what is left of mankind will come together in a psychic age and realize together the power and potential of the spirit. This will be an age of beauty and tranquility before immortality. We are the embryo of eternal love. Soon we must learn how to emerge.

I now believe that the spiritual or sentient part of man is part of a Being, power, or force of infinite love and beauty, immortal and immeasurable by any known human physical senses. I am here for a purpose and will have many, multiple purposes before I am completely assimilated.

God is part of me and I am part of Him. My physical being is only the vehicle of my soul.

Man stands between microcosm and macrocosm; we exist in creation and everything in creation exists in us. Life is within us, yet most of us look for it from the outside.

We change when we find love.
We change when we find death.

Chapter Five

PHILOSOPHY AND PARAPSYCHOLOGY

Years have now passed since my first mystical out-of-body experience. I have read and studied volumes on ESP and parapsychological subjects, sifting and seeking what I can accept as truth. The scientist is very deep and complex in his search and it takes at least a college level knowledge of math, physics and chemistry to follow. He ultimately arrives at the same place as theologists, who have been sitting there for centuries.

I shall attempt to simplify the facts I have learned. Seeking ESP or parapsychological knowledge is similar to seeking a path to God through science. Parapsychology is the study of 1) information received which cannot be explained by our known sense organs, 2) the influence of the human mind on physical phenomena.
Parapsychology takes in many fields. Due to the nature of many strange examples of psychic phenomena, they are difficult to investigate and prove credible through scientific facts. The lack of physical proof results in a large segment of "I don't believe" people.

Previous to my near-death experience I sought the answer to "after death, what?" I could not accept what the Bible, ministers, priests and rabbis said, with their great ecclesiastical differences. Is there a heaven or hell, or do I just lose my identity and that is the end? Now I believe that when death occurs, the soul takes leave and functions.

Who am I? Why am I here? Where am I going? What is the meaning of life? What is the nature of man?

These are not easy questions that can be answered simply or systematically. Each of us must ultimately face the truth of our existence. Our realm of personal experiential knowledge is the life situation of our "selves." Life is experience. We must exist, love, and return our life to God when the time comes.

Your philosophy of life must change with your living. What is the meaning of your existence? Why are you here? Your search must be an individual odyssey. You can listen to others, but in the end you must find your own answers. There is nothing more upsetting than the loss of a belief that you have retained all your life. You have to unlearn and then relearn, then discover that what you were taught is no longer true.

A large portion of our thinking is need oriented. Subjective factors guide us. Value judgements are important. You must play fair with your experience (especially an NDE) if you want your judgement respected.

When phenomena contradict the laws of physics, open-minded people feel an intellectual discomfort. I've heard people comment in the discussion of psychic phenomena: "It is the kind of thing I would not believe in even if it is true." Believe me, there are many documented, unbelievable experiences. Seeing and experiencing a fact that is contrary to most standard beliefs does not alter the belief or fact. The will to disbelieve does not alter the belief or fact. The will to disbelieve is greater than the will to believe, in most people.

It is like the story of the white crow. It is a common fact that all of the multi-millions of crows in the world are black. But what if a group of us saw a white crow? One white crow out of multi-millions of black would not change the general statement, "All crows are black." The sighting by any small group compared to the multi-millions of people who believe "all crows are black" would also not statistically alter the fact in any measurable way. So it seems to be with ESP; a small group sees, documents, and contradicts a known fact. Like the ripple caused by a stone thrown into a pond, it soon quiets and is absorbed in the greater body.

It is hard to realize that our physical body is only a carrier for our inner or spiritual body: a counterpart body of spiritual energy. What inner body? Show me something that I don't have to accept on faith alone. Believe it or not, this has been accomplished in the laboratories of parapsychologists in different areas of the world. Our bodies have a definite force field which can now be measured with instruments similar to electric encephalograms and electrocardiograms. There is a definite form of energy which we do not know much about yet. It reminds me of electricity – we still do not know of its exact definition, but we have learned how to harness and use it. I think that very shortly we will find a similar situation with ESP.

I am trying to report on some of the more interesting aspects of parapsychology without becoming too technical. I find that most writers on these subjects either become so technical that they are hard to follow, or else write so sensationally that they are difficult to believe.

One of the most sensational subjects in the field of parapsychology is what is called an out-of-body experience (OBE). There are many documented stories of people being seen when they were physically miles away by people who have no reason to be doubted. The word "ghosts" tends to scare most of us. There is no reason for fear; we just lack knowledge. Why should an apparition be different from the physical-bodied person we knew? What makes us think that they are any smarter or emotionally changed from what they were? In many cases a bond of love exists between people, which enables the non-material being to appear.

Those who have experienced out-of-body happenings report that they have a second body that floats out and they have a flying sensation. They can almost instantly transport from one place to another. I have personally talked to and have been told some fascinating events in other people's lives. Danger or stress seem to accentuate these happenings.

For those who desire some scientific correlation, one of many examples happened in 1965 at the University of California at Los Angeles. A professor of psychology tested a young woman who had the ability to leave her body. She was placed in a closed room that had only a couch and an observation window. An EKG and cardiograph were attached to her body. On a shelf near the ceiling, way beyond her physical reach, a random five digit number was placed. After going into a trance-like state, she was able to leave her body and read this number. The odds are 100,000 to one against guessing the correct number. Significant changes took place in the brain wave and cardiogram patterns at this time.

Similar experiments are being conducted by scientists around the world. They are searching for answers based on scientific facts. They are studying what is called an altered state of consciousness. The mind does have some type of space or energy that exists independent of the physical body. Religious leaders call this the soul.

My experience leads me to believe that the laws of science, as presently known, do not hold true and cannot be used to measure certain so-called psychic phenomena. In a supernatural realm, human words and concepts are not adequate for description and definitions. It is hard to discard some of what we have been taught from childhood as a measuring stick, but maybe in another realm our scientific premises will not hold true.

A multi-dimensional world is hard to comprehend. Suppose we live in a two-dimensional world (as in a flat picture) and a three-dimensional being (as we are now) visited us. We would see only the part that was in flat contact with our world. Now, take us into a three-dimensional world and have a four-dimensional being visit us. What do you think we would see? Who knows? Our present senses in our visible world cannot comprehend the complete supernatural realm.

Chapter Six

PSYCHOKINESIS

Psychokinesis (PK) or telekinesis is a description of a phenomenon, not an explanation. It is the movement of physical objects with no physical source of power. There are many terms and theories but no one really knows where the power comes from or too much about it. It could be a biological force or mental energy. It is basically an unconscious process. The ability of the mind to exert and influence ordinary matter, causing it to move unnaturally, defying the laws of physics, is fascinating and awesome.

PK is one of a variety of interrelated phenomena termed paranormal or psychic. It can occur spontaneously, but some of the more dramatic episodes focus at time of death. For example, it is reported that a clock started or stopped at a dramatic moment. A time of crisis seems to stimulate ESP. Poltergeist disturbances are thought to be a form of PK.

Some psychics and mediums have the power to move and levitate objects. They are able to materialize quasi-physical phantoms from ectoplasm, a psycho-biological force. We need more scientific investigation in this field.

Psychokinetic ability is not as uncommon as you would imagine. People with this ability have been seen on TV programs and have been viewed by millions moving inanimate objects without trickery. Uri Geller is perhaps the most publicized in this field. He was tested under laboratory conditions at Stanford Research Institute of California (1972), and found to have tremendous psychic power. He can cause metals to bend, and raise thermometer temperatures by mental concentration, amongst other phenomena. Unfortunately, he is also a showman and some of his stage performances have come under a cloud of suspicion.

Nina Kulagina, a Russian woman, has done many bizarre things. She has been filmed many times and investigated by the most prominent of Russian scientists. Common objects placed on a table – bread, matches, cigarettes, etc. – are made to move off. No trickery. Her brain waves become 50 times greater than normal. Her heartbeat increases 150 to 240 beats per minute and actual physical weight loss occurs. She has been tested under laboratory and scientific controls. Others who have this ability have also been documented and recorded. Our known laws of physics are inadequate for explanation.

The Spiritualist movement, which was popular before World War I and declined afterwards, seems to have been responsible for bringing to light mediums and people vested with the gift of ESP and PK. At that time many investigations were made, both scientific and non-scientific, and evidence gives some support to this movement.

Cycles of human interest in paranormal subjects rise and decline with the times. At present, the most publicized events seem to be the near-death experiences. What is the relationship between mediums and life after death? Mediumship has declined compared to what it was in the past. But publicity about people who have this strange ability leaks out of the laboratories and becomes sensationalized.

Professor Inyuskin (Russia) advanced the theory that all living things generate an atomic structure of "counter energy" which builds a duplicate physical system within the organism (he calls this a bioplasmic body), which radiates energy and creates life fields. This is an interesting theory supported more by conjecture than scientific evidence.

When phenomena that defy physical explanation occur, it leads to conjecture that maybe there is a deeper association between life and human consciousness than we comprehend. Obviously, we do not know enough about PK to explain it under any of our known laws of physics. The unconscious mind has a will that can be used to direct and manipulate PK without the conscious mind knowing it.

For what good can this force be used? If it can move objects, maybe it can be used to move cells and tissues to help regenerate the body's healing process. People who heal by "laying on of hands" may have some of this power. The consensus of opinion seems to be that PK is the force, unique to living organisms, which encompasses many other forces. Perhaps it is a pure mental force started by will power? The subject is so complex, with so many theories, that no one is able to explain how it works by measurable scientific standards. Is it a biological force or a type of material energy which allows mind and matter to interact? Is it a part of a cosmic energy permeating all matter? There are many theories and much more to be done before we can come up with an answer acceptable to our scientific community.

Poltergeistism (PG) is the scientific name for objects mysteriously moving and flying about in so-called haunted areas. It is sort of a subdivision of psychokinetic energy. Newspapers and books have reported these happenings for centuries. Exorcists, mediums and psychics have been involved in trying to stop or remove these phenomena with various degrees of success and failure. Very little is known scientifically about PG, with the exception of extensive research showing that it exists.

Chapter Seven

PERSONAL EXPERIENCES

Evil Apparition

A great many years have passed and I still have a vivid memory of an experience when I was two or three years old. One day my mother took me to visit my grandmother, who lived on the top floor of an old brick building in a suburb of Boston. The apartment, what was described in those days as a railroad flat, had a long hall with the parlor at one end and the kitchen at the other. Off the hall were living rooms, bedrooms, and a large bathroom.

The memory of the old bathroom is very clear. It contained an old sink on legs, an old-fashioned bathtub, a water closet with a wooden box above, and a flush chain hanging down. On one side was a large air shaft, about six feet across, with a window facing the kitchen window.

The apartment was three stories high. The bathroom door had an old-fashioned key for privacy. Like all toddlers, I was curious, played with the key, and inadvertently locked myself in. After a short while, when the adults realized I was not around, they shook and banged on the door. They panicked and called the fire department.

While this was going on, beneath the sink, staring at me, was a large, coal-black dog. Wide open jaws showed large canine teeth. Saliva drooled from the hanging tongue. The eyes were horrible. Fiery red, like two burning coals, they were hypnotically fascinating.

Half a century later, during my near-death experience, I saw similar eyes when I perceived the hooded apparitions moving off to infinity, their spirits emanating a tortured wailing. But a toddler, even one with a locked vision staring at these fiery red orbits, was too young to feel fear.

At this moment the air shaft window opened with a crash, as a fireman had put a ladder across from the kitchen to crawl over. The horrible apparition in the form of a dog vanished. When I emerged with the fireman, I was scolded for locking the door. I tried to tell them about the dog in the bathroom, but no one paid attention to me.

On the bottom floor of this old building was a small grocery and shoe repair store. A dank, dark, never-used cellar lay beneath; containing no windows and an earthen floor. The air shaft terminated there.

What was the apparition I had seen? Where did it originate? After seventy years why is this memory so vivid?

I have never told this story before because it is so weird I was afraid it would be unbelievable.

Tales of an Apparition and Psychic Inheritance

England, 1943, early in World War II. I am a soldier stationed near London. I become friendly with a lovely English girl, Netty, who is serving in the Army Territorial Service, which is similar to our WACS. German bombers are having a picnic with indiscriminate bombing every night. Netty is on fire watch on the roof of a large building in London. Incendiary bombs set the building on fire and she is in great danger, not knowing how she can escape. Flames are everywhere. Suddenly her father, who has been dead for many years, appears. He says, "Don't be afraid, girl; follow me." He shows her a way out that saves her life.

Her family has lived on the Scottish border for generations, going back to the time of King Arthur, and they have always had a psychic affinity. When I asked if she had seen her father before she answered, "many times." She then told me the following story.

While she was home on leave sometime previous, she was in the basement helping her mother with the laundry. A window at ground level overlooked the garden. She was near the window doing the wash while her mother was in the rear with her back to her. Netty looked out. It was a clear sunny day. There was her father walking in the garden, smoking his pipe. She uttered one word, "Mother!" Her mother turned and said, "My God, it's father!" They watched for a few moments until he faded away.

Here were two people who saw the same thing at the same time with no suggestive communication between them.

For generations there existed a psychic affinity in her family. It was a tradition that their oldest son went to sea. Once years back her aunt, who lived with them, woke them all in the middle of the night. She said there had been a bad accident and Jim, the son, had been hurt. The wall in her room had opened up and she was able to see a strange scene which she described vividly. The ship was unloading at a port in India. Suddenly the cargo net parted and the contents hit Jim, who was standing underneath. He was rushed to the hospital.

The next day they received a telegram stating that there had been an accident but that Jim was going to be all right.

Many months later, when Jim came home, she told him what she had seen. She described everything vividly – the ship, the cargo, what he and the others were wearing, how many sailors and how many Hindus there were – every little detail about the docks. All of it was confirmed by Jim.

How can we explain this story by any of the logical laws of science we have in the present day?

Chapter Eight

RELATED ESP PHENOMENA

How about thinking of some object or picture and having that thought develop as a picture on an unexposed photographic film? We call this phenomena psychic photography, and any public library will have books with pictures galore of psychics who have this special ability. Ted Serios, one of the most widely known in this field, has been tested time and again under laboratory conditions and was able to project mental images onto film. Again, no real explanation.

Spirit photography has also been documented. When developed, a photo shows an extra image. For example, a photo of a horse showed a boy who had been dead for four years. The boy had a strong love for animals.

When wedding pictures of a girl's marriage to a soldier were developed they showed a sailor in his place, a man she had secretly married a few years back. He had died.

Sir Arthur Conan Doyle, author of *Sherlock Holmes*, appeared in a photo two years after his death.

How powerful is the mind? What are the latent possibilities for the future if mankind is allowed to develop? Have we an astral or energy body that duplicates the physical body? If we have, then the secrets of ESP could be related to the astral body. What evidence supports this?

ESP Magazine of March, 1977, contains a report on an apparition called "Myra." She was contacted by a group at the University of Missouri called SORRAT – Society for Research on

Rapport and Telekinesis. Myra was a student at the University of Missouri in Columbus, Missouri, who died in 1860. Records were researched. She was photographed with her cooperation, using an infra-red camera, at 11:20 P.M. on June 27, 1967, in front of the university building. The picture is a clear image of a lovely young woman – however, there is no shadow (SORRAT, J.T. Richards).

Kirlian photography, which is high frequency photography, shows a bio-luminescence effect surrounding the body, similar to an aura. Many people with psychic ability can see the luminescence on their own and interpret the variety of colors emanating from the body. When a person who has had an amputation has a Kirlian photograph made, the whole body part appears, not only on human beings, but on any cellular living objects. In Russia (1968) three scientists at the State University published a paper stating "All living things, plants, animals, humans, not only have a physical body of atoms and molecules but also a counterpart body of energy." Many books of technical evidence support this statement. Again, photographs of the Kirlian technique can be found in any public library, for anyone who wants to delve further into this field.

Psychic Surgery or psychic healing is another of the more sensational aspects of the psychic field. Would anyone believe that a human being could be cut open with a knife, feel no pain, have a portion of the body removed, not bleed, and be instantly cured? Arigo, a man in Brazil recently deceased, had the power to perform such surgeries. Arigo was examined during these feats by many doctors and medical specialists. They filmed and photographed operations such as sticking a knife into a patient's eye and removing a cataract, with the patient feeling no pain. One examining doctor, Henry Puharich, M.D., Northwestern University, an ardent disbeliever at first, states that he was personally operated on in a matter of seconds with no measurable sensation. His would have been a lengthy operation under modern surgical techniques. He was unable to explain it. Again, books and pictures of hundreds of operations performed by

Arigo are available.

The type known as Philippine Surgery has come under much questioning. The practitioners use only their hands, pushing them (so it seems) through the skin for removal of various organs. Some feats reported are unbelievable and are probably trickery.

Manual healers, who heal by touching or the placing on of hands, are fairly common. It is thought that they have the ability to accelerate the natural healing process of the body, but no one really knows the answer. Modern medicine does not understand the full range of psychosomatic effects. Can anyone explain the religious miracles of healing that take place at Lourdes and various shrines around the world? These have been verified by well-known doctors and theologians. Why is it not possible for this divine power to be tapped by a few gifted people?

Sai Baba, a man living today in a remote village in India, has a divine power. He is imbued with the real spirit of God, similar to Jesus, Moses, Allah, and other great religious leaders. Scientists who have met him and seen his work call him a true avatar, an example of how man may develop thousands of years in the future. He is clairvoyant, telepathic, a healer and teacher. He can materialize objects from nothing. He transcends the laws of physics and science. Eminent doctors and scientists who have seen him state, "It cannot be, yet it is." He seeks no personal gain but preaches God's love. His teachings are the epitome of all religions combined: goodness and spiritual love.

"You, a body, mind or soul, are a dream. What you really are is existence, knowledge and bliss. You are part of God, and God is part of you." (from Sai Baba)

I have talked to several people who have made a pilgrimage to meet Sai Baba, and I have seen movies taken by them. Several books have been written, one of the most impressive was by an American psychiatrist. Is the world ready for Sai Baba's messages of love any more than they were for any of the great religious leaders of the past?

Eminent doctors and psychologists are now investigating, scientifically, practices that have been in use since ancient times in India. They are being correlated and corroborated with our present-day knowledge as much as possible. Perhaps the most interesting is the theory of kundalini, an energy contained in the lower spine of the body. When awakened and channeled correctly, it allows one to merge with the cosmic consciousness. The mysteries of the universe are ultimately unfolded.

This is not as far out as it may seem. Scholars are wondering if the kundalini theory explains the energy that is responsible for the near-death experiences that are now being reported.

Through meditation and various Yoga practices kundalini energy, contained near the base of the spine, is drawn out to the various chakras of the body (a chakra is a subtle energy center in the body; seven of them are usually recognized in Eastern religions). All life is considered as one, governed by the same forces on a macro and micro level. Everything is interrelated and inseparable. To activate and control this energy, gurus spend years in meditative practice.

An interesting aspect is the way sex can be used to transform energy. Sex in the cosmic plane is thought to be a fusion of polarities – not intercourse. Mortal sex is seen as a divine, vital energy which is able to influence the physio-psychic state to rise to a higher cosmic plane.

When kundalini energy is aroused, supernatural powers are possible. Even gravity can be defied and out-of-body experiences and cosmic travels are experienced. Novices should not get involved with kundalini energy, as there are psycho-physical dangers here.

Further research into the question of "Who am I?" brings us to what is called channeling, a term used to explain a phenomena through which people receive messages from a personality not of this world. The person who receives is often called a true medium, sensitive, or channel who has supernormal faculties due to a detachment of the subconscious mind. This allows the subconscious to attain knowledge without using the usual sense organs. In a trance the conscious mind is inactive and the unconscious mind predominates.

In 1833 an amazing clairvoyant or medium, Daniel Douglas Home, was born. For 25 years his manifestations and astonishing feats were seen and documented by people of unblemished integrity. He had the power of levitation, could float up to the ceiling, float out one window and enter another, cause a grand piano to float in the air, and perform many other feats that defy any scientific explanation. Again, it seems, "It cannot be and yet it is." A famous scientist of the time, Sir William Crooks, investigated Home and said, "I didn't say it was possible, I said it was true."

We like to say that most unknown phenomena can be explained in terms of unrecognized powers of the human mind. Yet we can explain a large portion only by means of the theory of a spiritual hypothesis, a disembodied intelligence. A study of the medical cases of multiple personalities exhibiting knowledge beyond what they have ever learned, lends credence to this theory.

People who pursue the subject of disembodied intelligence have been called gullible idiots by those with closed minds. Yet how else can we seek truth? There are so many documented stories of unbelievable psychic happenings that why so many deny their existence is incomprehensible. In every case in which a skeptic has delved and studied, he has become a convert to the "life-after-death" theory.

There is a paranormal intelligence existing beyond our normal reality. Many interesting books and philosophies have been written by people in contact with this intelligence. As often occurs in the parapsychological field, some channels or mediums have used fakery and showmanship. This has hurt legitimate scientific investigation into the field. Ultimate reality must take into accord more than our five senses can interpret.

At a place called Findhorn in England, a New Age group got together and demonstrated the power of good that could come from channeling. Human cooperation with the spirits of nature created some outstanding documented results.

Man's spiritual sense is awakening. Guidance is needed. Maybe channels are part of a coming New Age. Reason plus intuition may help our judgements.

Many astral beings who communicate through channels state that we are living, spiritual beings in this universe heading towards an eventual union with the One God, who is the underlying identity of "all that is."

Spiritualism is the science, philosophy and religion of continuous life based on the fact of communication via mediums or channels with the spirit world. Spiritualism removes the fear of death and teaches personal responsibility. Death is a change of conditions; life is eternal; man is a soul that has a body; as ye sow, so shall ye reap. The soul progresses through the ages to levels where God is love and love is God.

In searching for knowledge, we must investigate all alternative sources of information or guidance. There is more to existence than the dimension of space and time to which we are accustomed.

Chapter Nine

PERSONAL THOUGHTS AND QUOTES

For thousands of years technological advances by mankind have been very slow. In ten million years of mankind, one generation has seen man go from the horse and buggy to space travel. My father rode a horse; my son can ride a spaceship. Electricity, autos, planes, television and medical advances that save and prolong lives are taken for granted. A heart transplant doctor would have been burned at the stake as a sorcerer a few centuries past. What has caused this sudden influx of knowledge at this period of time? Why now?

The mass of phenomena called "mystical" has been treated with scientific disregard and contempt. Psychology, physiology, and medicine turn away and use the phrase "effects of the imagination." History records this phenomena under many names: trances, possessions, miracles, etc.

There are more than 100 million planets in 100 million galaxies. Why not life existing elsewhere in other forms? If our body is only a carrier for our spirit, why could not another form of life do the same?

We have all been steeped in pure physical science, so it may be difficult to understand how psychic laws differ from physical.

When a psychic event supersedes a physical impossibility, people call it a miracle. We have only a vague understanding of the workings of the psychic universe, and what we do understand forces us to completely reevaluate that which we were taught in ordinary physics. What laws can explain something like a near-death experience or mental telepathy?

Parapsychologists are looking for explanations. First, the phenomenon to be investigated must be real, not hearsay or imaginative, to be investigated scientifically; but how far can we go when our scientific laws don't conform? Where do mystics fit in?

Interstellar space may contain certain organisms that are as at home in their space environment as we are native to earth. The atoms that we consist of were synthesized in stars that are now dead. Can mind and intelligence exist without the hindrance of matter? Maybe upon death the mind leaves matter like a butterfly leaves a cocoon.

Planets are to civilizations what rivers are to salmon – spawning places. When we become spiritually adult, we will have to go out into the sea of space and accept our place in the cosmological community. In the etheric or astral planes there are many levels of attainment, each an advance.

It is difficult to accept a new thought to displace old dogmas that you have been taught all your life. Test a new idea and be tested by it. Sometimes studying a drop of water may yield the secrets of the ocean.

To an earthworm travelling through the dense medium of solid packed earth, a fish swimming in water is as incomprehensible as a bird floating freely in the air is to the fish. Spiritual life existing in a space-time medium is just as difficult for mankind to comprehend. Therefore, many deny the possibility of its existence. Evidence is often explained away rather than explored.

Are we a living part of God, as a corpuscle or living cell is part of us – a small function adding to the whole? Is our purpose the gathering of knowledge through experience or mental ability? To whom does God pray? Is this life the ultimate; are thoughts of further life incomprehensible? Those who dare venture beyond the known are almost always misunderstood.

A bodiless personality is hard to conceive. We have a body image based on medical facts at the sensory level. The question is: If we have a non-physical body, of what does it consist? The occult claims the physical body is a sensory illusion and that there is a phantom body that interpenetrates the physical.

If this ailing civilization is to be healed of its contagious selfishness and greed, there must be an appreciation for the fact that every individual is an essence, an immortal soul, accountable for its own actions, who will endure to face the positive and negative consequences of all he does or fails to do. Doing something useful for mankind should be the dominant factor of life. Good work done in this life augments good in the next. Evil impedes the progress of your soul in future lives. Advancement after death depends first on your progress on earth. Love and service create a universal warmth and immediate advancement.

Man is given free will but is held accountable as to how it has been used.

Plato years ago pointed out that if we envision a wise and fulfilling future, the better is the chance that our dreams will become realities. We have to trade benefits to ourselves for benefits to the next generation for mankind to survive. Society can survive only by the present generation sacrificing for future generations. Where is evolution taking us? Are we going to be a super race? At present we cannot resolve this question. The potential is unlimited.

Sociologically, we have not kept pace with science, but have retrogressed. Genghis Khan killed by the thousands, Adolf Hitler by the millions. Crime is rampant, social mores practically non-existent. Millions are starving in a world that has food surpluses. The prime word of every religion is "Thou shall not kill," but even in the name of religion, we slaughter one another.

How long is God going to allow this? Every civilization tells of a great catastrophe, flood, earthquake, fire, "the sun standing still." For the sun to stand still, the earth must stop rotating. The earth is wobbling on its axis right now, and a small polar shift will tip it. There is evidence galore that this happened many times previously and can easily happen again. We blithely ignore scientific evidence and go merrily on our way with the thought, "It can't happen to me."

Why not? Are we different from our ancestors who thought the same before they perished? Some very advanced civilizations have risen and fallen since time immemorial. Most of them seem to have been destroyed during a morally decadent period.

Is it possible that a new world is coming following the destruction of the old, a world where psychic values will be developed as technology reigned in the old, where perhaps the words, "Do unto others as you would have them do unto you," will become the law of the land? I wonder what it would be like if in the future we lived in a psychic society where we would know one another's inner feelings and state of mind. Lies and dishonesty would disappear. This might be the nucleus of an Olympian Earth.

Why is it that we are afraid of cancer, diseases, and great catastrophes, and yet human scavengers from Hitler to Kublai Khan can have such ecstatic followers?

Do good, become close to people and the human race, and you will become closer to God. What will you say when you are asked what you have done with life to benefit the world?

Something must be done. Man must propose, or else God will dispose.

It is hard for any mortal to visualize God: a blinding incandescent matter of pure energy, total intelligence and love, of which we are all a particle. This is why mankind has always worshipped God's messengers – Jesus, Mohammed, Buddha, Moses, and all the other countless prophets or leaders from pagan times to the present. Since they have our own physical form, we find it easier to relate to them. We have the tendency to reject, to be unable to comprehend anything alien, anything that deviates from our own personal, normal environment. Many find it difficult to have a reverence for an intelligence of a different form or species. We are not emotionally prepared for an extraterrestrial intelligence. The Biblical answer of God, "I AM," is enough for a great many. We are all part of God; God is part of us, therefore, all mankind is our brother.

Life contains many varied roads of travel. Each must find his own way. The path is not as important as the direction. Whether we learn from passages of the Bible, Koran, Torah or Vedas, the important thing is that we understand that the spiritual life transcends the human span. Many paths leading to one alter.

Man is a soul that has a body, not a body that has a soul. There is no religion in the world after death. All religions teach us to love one another. Your coming position depends on your character, on the good deeds you have performed on earth. Good thoughts and deeds are what count. We are all here for God's purpose. It does not matter how we worship or what we believe. What we truly are is what counts.

God in all religions tells us to love our fellow beings. How many of us pay heed to these words? We are consumed by the everyday business of living, but our subconscious mind forgets nothing. We are not all that we were meant to be.

"God is the good in everyone and the good in everyone is God."

I have come to the realization that all gods are one God. I believe in all religions and no religion. Take away our modern technology and scientific knowledge and there is no difference between us and our ancestors. Have we really advanced any distance on the pathway to the stars?

Wonderment about the purpose of this existence and the unknown future is the common thread of most philosophers of both the past and the present. Marcus Aurelius of ancient Greece could step into any modern college philosophy department and tell us more about life and death than the teachers of today.

Philosophers, educators, prophets, messiahs, all preach and

discuss the ethics of life. What is the inherent trait in mankind that prevents us from leading the "good life?" Is there a counter-balance to good called evil that swings out of control so easily? Does every one step forward necessitate two steps backward? I once thought education was the answer, but have since seen that many of the well-educated use their knowledge and science for the wrong purposes. Love, truth, and justice are needed to unite humanity.

Evil is something we create with our own thoughts and actions, deeds done to enhance our own physical importance, and is destroyed by good deeds and loving kindness. We must understand ourselves to be able to conceive the idea of God and future existence relative to religion.

When we leave our bodies at death, we are not impaired by anything physical as we now see it. As a short wavelength like an X-ray or radio wave can pass through solid matter, so can our spirits. We exist in a different time dimension. Science, philosophy and metaphysics blend together at death. Studies show that as we approach death closely there is a great calmness and serenity. Denying that there is no existence before birth or after death contradicts an essential law of physics – the conversion of energy: matter can be neither created or destroyed, but only transformed. Life is a process of transformation.

Can you say you are the same person at 50 that you were at 15? Or 30? Though you are of the same name, you are composed of many different personalities as you evolve through time. Rebirth is the continuing on of a process, rather than the changing of a substance. Future personality is affected by mental status at time of death.

What is a "SOUL?" No one really knows, as there is no clear definition, but it is thought to be "an ego entity that exists independent of the physical body and survives after the physical end." It makes up the psychic side of us and is thought to consist of all consciousness, mind, and character of a person. Many scientists evade the question of a soul, saying maybe there is a cord of energy that leaves at death, but call this "esoteric speculation." Even though many of them believe in a spiritual out-of-body existence, many do not. Unless they can put their fingers on it in a laboratory, they pass. The soul cannot be analyzed in a test tube, yet it cannot be denied.

The philosophies of the East are soul-oriented, while most Western philosophies are body-oriented; spiritualistic as opposed to materialistic. Researchers stay within a domain of scientific mathematical rules, and if a soul does not follow the laws of biology and physics as we know them, they refuse to draw any conclusions. There are many scientific ostriches who bury their heads in the familiar sands of conformity. They refuse to accept facts that do not fit into preconceived pigeon-holes of what they think ought to be, blindly rejecting what is. Where does science end and philosophy begin?

Everyone wants to go to heaven but no one wants to die to get there. Everyone wants to know the answers to the great mystery of what happens when our physical body quits. Do we meet God? What is He like? Do we have a body? Will we meet people we knew on earth? What is our relationship to them? Will we remember our past life? How about sex? Is there a hell? Is heaven a pleasant place? What do we do there? How does religion figure in? – and a myriad more questions.

There must be a definite answer to all these questions, but if I or anyone else were to attempt to answer, would you believe? What would *you* demand or require as proof? If a man you met said, "Hello, I am Jesus Christ," what would you require as proof? Would you walk away thinking "this is a nut," or would you think "maybe I ought to invite him for dinner." What would you require as proof?

"Seeing is believing" is not a scientifically reliable basis of judgement. Believe in what you understand, not what you see. To the naked eye the stars above appear to be about the size of a dime, but we know through astronomy that many of them are larger than our own sun.

"According to scientists" is the biggest bugaboo and brow-beating statement that prefaces a sentence that may or may not be true. Scientific premises may change daily. Today's fantasy is tomorrow's fact. Science is so mysteriously endowed to some people that simply to say "according to modern scientific discoveries..." is to invest what follows with authority. This makes possible the presentation of fabrications as truth. Some scientifically proven facts of today would have been rejected as fantasy a hundred years ago and condemned as witchcraft two hundred years ago.

One school of thought is that the mind is completely different from the brain. It is non-physical; the brain is physical. Thought does not conform to ordinary laws; the brain follows the laws of chemistry and physics. The body ages; the mind matures. Consciousness changes with knowledge and experience, so the mind is not the same at various age levels.

There are various stages of progression as we advance spiritually in the afterlife. Each one has an entry phase, a development period, and a preparation period for the next stage. There is the earth experience; the stage immediately after death; then the intermediate plane or evaluation, which turns into the plane of light and timelessness. These are of an advanced spiritual nature, the essence of creativity. There is no earth vocabulary to describe them, as they are not contained in any earthly octave. Thought is the expression; words are obsolete. Your own school of thought will be the result of what you read, study and believe. The soul struggles and labors ever upward from one plane to another, knowing ecstasy and sorrow, but not as it did on earth.

The ultimate goal is to assimilate with our Creator and become part of a blinding essence of pure thought. There is a great deal more to this, but now we are in a spiritualistic medium realm. Today's researchers will go as far as the portal of future existence, and there they stop.

It is difficult to comprehend other modes of existence if we use only earth senses. There are many other senses, some called extra-sensory, that must be taken into account. If our spiritual body after death consists of energy of different extra-low frequency wavelengths, why should it be difficult to comprehend our passing through a solid medium similar to the way X-rays or radio waves do? Can you comprehend a spiritual man existing in the vast cosmos of what we call space? Our inability to see anything but material phenomena blinds us to the fact that spiritual and cosmic energy is in progress at all times, all around us.

There is much more to be known and studied of the "world beyond death." Knowledge will wipe out the dread and threat of death. The frenzy to gain material things will be diminished and replaced by the true values of life and love.

> "At ebb tide I wrote
> a line upon the sand
> and gave it all my heart
> and all my soul.
> At flood tide I returned
> to read what I had inscribed
> and found my ignorance upon the shore."
>
> Kahil Gibran

Chapter Ten

REINCARNATION

According to the theory of reincarnation something of the person persists, the personality or individuality, from one earth life to another. It is similar to the rings of a cut tree, one layer surrounding the next for each life.

Life before birth is similar to life after death. In a person's evolution birth and death are continuous. This is a commonly accepted belief by many of the world's religions today. People who have experienced reincarnation, whether by hypnotic regression or channeling, speak of a homecoming. Loss of fear of death is a common factor, similar to the feelings of those who have had a near-death experience.

All religions believe in the existence of the soul and the repeated quest for salvation. From the ancient Egyptians and Greeks to the Hindus and Buddhists, the soul is considered a pre-existing entity which takes up residence in a succession of bodies, becoming carnal and then astral, reincarnating time after time.

Reincarnation has been a matter or belief or disbelief. Either accept the facts or, like many, reject them because you don't like what they imply. The basic idea is that you die and return again to another physical body, live again, die again, and return again any number of times.

My thought is that this is not an indefinite process but only a continuity until the spirit attains a goal of perfection which permits it to pass to the next higher plane, whether it takes a thousand or a hundred thousand years as we measure time.

Ancient Indian (Vedic) and Egyptian religions believe in transmigration of the soul, which is not the same as reincarnation. They believe that the soul goes into an animal form and gradually develops up the ladder of existence for purification.

The physical body changes every moment; growth and old age are taking place constantly, but the spiritual soul exists permanently. This is the difference between matter and spirit. The body changes, the soul is eternal. It reincarnates into new material bodies, giving up old and useless ones.

Life force is an energy field. Remember, a basic law of physics is "energy can be neither created nor destroyed, only transformed." Therefore at death energy must continue to exist in some form.

I think we are a continuing entity and that we return again and again to the physical form to execute the prime law of the universe – love – that we learn and absorb from the spiritual side. Physical form is a test. We are all one, and a part of God. The way to spiritual success depends on the good we do for mankind without hope of reward or self gratification.

Regressive hypnosis is perhaps the most factual way of proving other existences. There are thousands of documented cases of other lives. Some become sensational, as the Bridey Murphy case, others more mundane. More readers are interested only in the strangeness and sensationalism of the stories. How and where did the subjects obtain the knowledge and language of countries to which they had no access in their lifetime?

The director of a division of parapsychology, a professor of psychiatry, Dr. Ian Stevenson, has assessed and investigated more than 1600 cases of reincarnation. He is only one of many, many investigators. He has written a text called *Twenty Cases Suggestive of Reincarnation*. He has scientifically elucidated each case and has attacked his own premises from every angle. There is no doubt that these are true cases of reincarnation, yet the author uses the word "suggestive" in his title. This attitude is quite prevalent among scientists and people in important social positions. The minute they approach something esoteric, even though they believe a premise to be true, they back off. Are they paying homage to their social positions, afraid of ruffling their peers, or afraid because the answer does not conform to our present-day knowledge?

Throughout the ages there have been many documented cases of reincarnation, yet unless there is some sensational story that attracts publicity, Western religions cause us to ignore the subject.

Hypnotic Regression

I have a good friend with whom I have associated for many years. I rate him number one in the field of hypnosis and spiritual investigation. In his worldwide travels he has investigated and recorded unbelievable spiritual phenomena. I have been present and have helped him do many hypnotic regressions.

One evening I decided to try regression on myself. A knowledge of past lives has occurred to me many times. Scenes of another existence have come across my mind often when I have been in a meditative state. Once I was a medical priest in an ancient land before the existence of Egypt. I advanced in time to scenes of a desert oasis. Sand and palm trees surrounded me. Warm sun pleasured me. I saw myself sitting on pillows or cushions in front of a large desert tent. I was a person of some consequence. In another time, which I think was about 1000 A.D., I was a sailor and fisherman. A one-masted vessel was mine and I sailed in the area of the North Sea off the coast of England. I lost my life by drowning in a violent storm. I remember swimming towards a distant light on shore while lightning and thunder raged about me. I sank beneath the waves. At another time scenes of a merchant's life in Italy about 1400 A.D. create stirrings in my memory.

This time I decided to get a record of past experiences on tape, with the guidance of my hypnotist.

I definitely did not want to go through the memory of my near-death experience; I had a subjective fear of not coming back. We started, and gradually I felt myself sinking into a pitch-black void. The most terrible depressive feeling came over me, an actual physical fear. I have never felt so deeply depressed. All the sorrows of the world flowed through me. Tears and deep sobs racked my body. I struggled to return to consciousness. My hypnotist realized something was wrong and stopped the experiment. I have not had the courage nor the want to repeat this.

I am certain that I am a reincarnate, else how can I explain the various flashes of prior existences, the various visions of cities, dwellings, and scenes of which I had no previous knowledge? These are not hallucinations or dreams. There is no correlation to anything I have ever read or seen.

Somehow I feel, though I have no proof, that this is my last incarnation and that my next existence will be on another – and I hope higher – plane.

In Eastern religions, some of which go back to 4000 B.C., reincarnation plays an important role. Early Christian teachings gave the subject a greater importance that seems to have been deleted with time. The teachings on reincarnation by one of the great church fathers, the Roman philosopher Origen, became law when Constantine the Great converted his kingdom to Christianity in 308 A.D. The Nicean Council said reincarnation was a fact in 323 A.D.

Rebirth was believed by many early Christians. Origen taught it. Christ is quoted in the Gnostic scriptures (*Pistis Sophia*) as saying, "Souls are poured from one into another of different bodies of the world."

In 551 A.D. Emperor Justinian and his council condemned Origen, slaughtered those who differed and rewrote the Bible, deleting 36 to 40 books and all references to reincarnation. The Bible has been written again and again since that time, with different sayings and content. Following is a quotation from De Principis Origen (A.D. 185-254).

"The soul has neither beginning nor end... Every soul comes into this world strengthened by the victories or weakened by the defeats of its previous life. Its place in this world as a vessel appointed to honor or dishonor is determined by its previous merits or demerits. Its work in the world determines its place in the world which is to follow this."

Survival after physical death to most people means the existence of their personalities and memories and their relationships to others. In other words, a continuation of their identities without their bodies. But your personality is continually changing from birth to death, as you progress through life.

At death the soul enters a spaceless, timeless state where its last existence is evaluated (karma). Percipients in past life research speak and sometimes even write in ancient and foreign tongues, which is impossible for them to know in this present existence. Sex and race changes are common in the next incarnation. Reports from those who have been in a meta-conscious state in this realm between lives, called "bardo", state that they are judged, usually by a triumvirate of highly advanced spiritual souls. This has a great similarity to the Greek Triumvirate in mythology, the philosophy of Lao-Tzu, the Hindu Trimurti, and the Chrsitian Father, Son and Holy Ghost. This is when the past life is reviewed, evaluated, and recommendations are made for the next incarnation. This is the time when any emotional suffering you have caused to others is felt by you, and you come to the realization that the past is gone and you must atone in your struggle to reach the higher stages.

Xenoglossy is a term used to describe a situation in which a person, usually under hypnosis, speaks in a foreign tongue unknown to him, which cannot be explained away. A multitude of these cases are on tape, done by regressionists. One of the classics that has been investigated is the "Rosemary case" (Ref. A.S.P.R. Journal, Vol. XXVIII, 291). This is the story of an English girl who, under regression, states she lived in Egypt in 1380 B.C. as one of the wives of Pharaoh Amenhotep III. She speaks in a dead, practically unknown language, using correct idioms and phrases of that era. This was studied and confirmed by an eminent Egyptologist named Dr. Wood. Many, many cases on record are just as sensational, though controversial. Alien knowledge and aptitudes tend to show that there is another personality coexisting within. There are so many recorded and verified cases, many of them current, how can one disbelieve?

Thousands of cases of reincarnation have been published and can be found in any public library. These are not sensational stories, but are documented by psychological researchers in a field that is just coming to the forefront.

Cryptomnesia, "the remembrance of an early event later in life," can explain some stories that are similar to reincarnations. The subconscious retains an unbelievable amount of knowledge. Investigation is important before ruling on true reincarnation as against personality manifestations. One has to be careful of the many charlatans in this field who haven't the knowledge or skill to validate evidence.

Reincarnation is a cardinal teaching of most major religions in the world and is accepted by many thoughtful and intelligent people. The subconscious submerges the memory linkage between our past lives. Memory is still a tremendous mystery. Doctors try to lock it into the brain, psychologists say it is an integral part of personality, occultists link it to the ancient teachings of the astral body – a metaphysical plane. I think of them as similar to the ancient fable of the five blind men who went to visit an elephant.

The first man grasped the leg. "Why, an elephant is like a trunk," he exclaimed. The second touched his side. "Why, an elephant is like a wall," he exclaimed. The third touched his ear. "Why, an elephant is like a cabbage leaf," he exclaimed. The fourth touch his trunk. "Why, an elephant is like a snake," he exclaimed. The fifth touched his tail. "Why, an elephant is like a rope," he exclaimed. They were all partially correct.

Many people cannot accept the idea of reincarnation – strongly religious people with predetermined views, atheists who will not accept anything non-physical, philosophers who have accepted a particular philosophy, those with intellectual difficulties in accepting parts of the doctrine, spiritualists who have definite ideas of the hereafter, others who just don't like the idea of returning to earth.

The Hebrews rejected the concept since it projected the thought that the human race was not wholly dependent on their God.

Fundamentalist Christians reject reincarnation since it applies rebirth to all men, and not just through Jesus Christ. Episcopals, Universalists, and Unitarians are more open in their views. Most religions find it difficult to incorporate scientific findings and philosophies into their views.

Facts do not lie, but they can be interpreted in many different ways. With the same facts, priests, philosophers, and scientists come to many different conclusions, usually harmonious with their backgrounds.

Time

Reincarnation is a doctrine based on endless time cycles. Time is only a measurement for events. Events create time. No one knows for sure what time is. It is obvious that the subconscious is no respecter of time. Awareness can be of past, present or future. Time is not real, but only a mental tool we use for organizational purposes. It is a mental conception of our minds. Time does not flow, it just is. Past, present, and future can be one. For example, at a movie theater you can be in the middle of a picture, it is now. Take the film being projected and stretch it out. You can see the beginning, middle, and end all at the same time. Past, present, and future are now.

Absolute time or space cannot be measured except with an arbitrarily chosen frame in respect to one's self. The present moment contains past and future, and past within the future. Years are measurement of time for our earth life. When years or days are gone, they cannot be lived again. You build now for that time we call "forever" or "no time." The life of tomorrow is affected by the way you live your earth life.

Time is only an experience measuring the flow of our consciousness. Three different phenomena are evident.

1) Clock time, which measures space and the movement of the sun. It correlates events.
2) Subjective time, psychological or experiential. It is our individual experience of the continuum of our consciousness.
3) Matter in motion, or a sequence of events.

Humans experience the present, remember the past and anticipate the future. We are in time. God is timeless.

Being alive has many different meanings according to our powers of comprehension and levels of experience. We should cry at birth, not at death. Birth signifies the beginning of many years of tribulation and painful learning. Death is a release from our struggles, the beginning of freedom, beauty, and joy. The fear of death is greatly due to the fear of loss of personal identity – the fear that "I" will cease to be "me."

The time between transitions has had very little investigation compared with other parapsychological fields. Some researchers call it a "metaconscious state." Those who have experienced it have the same difficulty in trying to explain their experience as near-death experiencers. When people become one with universe, all sense of personal identity is lost. They are beyond space and time. They are part of existence itself.

Ancient races seemed to have a better grasp of this subject than modern man. They seemed to comprehend that a "life" between lives is our natural abode, from which we go forth to an arduous physical existence. The subject of reincarnation has been researched by many well-known scientists who have presented factual scientific evidence. Venturing into the unknown with stories that confound the common reason and logic of the current times creates furor and doubt. But so it has always been with those willing to take the first step forward into unknown territory.

In reincarnation regressions, the spirit seems to interact with the same entities regardless of the time factor in between. In the reincarnated state, family associations seem to be the same, but in a different relationship, depending upon the karmic necessity. Enlightenment comes only after many purifications of body, growth and development. People who have experienced rebirths seem to have the same difficulty as near-death experiencers in trying to express an inexpressible experience. They learn the "why" of their last existence. The soul is striving ever upward and this is the way it learns and strives to correct the errors of past existences. It is difficult to comprehend from an earthly view. The soul is in an ecstatic state of luminescence. There is no time element, only "now." Thought alone exists. There is no experience of existence without thought. Cosmic consciousness is a blinding light of bliss, ecstacy, and a tremendous permeating love.

Some subjects speak of "halls of learning, vast libraries, and seminar rooms." The learning process never ends. Each plane on the road to God-like perfection is lighter and brighter than the one before. Time spent between lives seems to vary, as reported by different researchers, from a short ten months to a long eight hundred years. The ancient Egyptians taught three thousand years. At present there is no probable answer. Time is only a yardstick of earthly measure.

Reincarnation regressions bring alive figures from the past, complete with their own memories and personalities. In hypnotic regression how does the unconscious get information that is so obscure and inaccessible that it takes weeks of research to uncover? Does a person under deep hypnosis become a sort of super medium and make contact with past spirits?

The Akashic theory holds that all records of all events are stored. The Akashic record is thought to be like a vast library of scrolls, housing all knowledge. You as an individual are thought of as a single scroll within the library, or as a single soul within the mind of God. During my own near-death experience a scroll-like, long parchment seemed to come from me and became part of the ethereal experience – a record of my entire life. Can a person under hypnosis make contact and access material from these scrolls?

The body's cells are constantly changing and dying. An adult body is completely different from a child's, yet the soul remains the same.

Advanced physics shows that a microscopic rebirth underlies everything in the physical world. Subatomic particles are constantly dying and being reborn. This same thing occurs in the macroscopic universe. Worlds are constantly dying and being reborn. You are not a body possessing a soul, you are a soul and own a temporary body. Originally the soul comes from God. We come from a spiritual world, but give this up to become material energy. We then are implanted in the cycle of life and death.

Once again, life has many different meanings according to our powers of comprehension and levels of experience. The usual pattern is one of gradual learning through many lives, gradual character strengthening, growth in integrity, charity and courage. With each new life a new brilliance is given the spirit and new values are added.

All past knowledge is dissolved when the spirit enters the earthly plane. Can people remember what they had for lunch last week or what clothes they wore? The knowledge is there, but can be brought forth only under hypnosis. There are many cases of children remembering past life experiences, usually when they are between the ages of two and five. In most cases this memory is lost as they grow older. A child develops a central identity which makes the present the only reality.

Reincarnation Memories of a Child

My wife is in the hospital in a terminally ill ward. She is dying of cancer. The attending personnel are wonderful, and specially trained. During the time I spend there I lecture on a forum for the nurses and relatives of other ill patients. I am hoping I can alleviate their fear of death by telling of my own experience. One evening a nurse tells me the following story and documents it after obtaining a promise that she will remain anonymous. It is the story of her son Adam, age two and a half in 1978, told in her own words.

"My sister and I took my son to the cemetery where my mother-in-law and father are both buried, to visit the grave sites. As we walked to the vicinity of my mother-in-law's grave, my son became emotionally upset. He insisted he wanted to leave. He kept crying, 'Let's go. Let's get out of here.' We didn't want to leave but he became so upset that we walked to our father's grave, instead. Suddenly he was acting fine. When we headed back to the car he started insisting that 'we go back that way.' He was referring to my mother-in-law's grave. He walked to the grave site and said, 'I was down there; I was dead.' Then he lay down on the ground, put his hands in a folded position over his chest, closed his eyes and said, 'Like this, I was dead.' He put two blades of grass in his nostrils and said, 'Like the tubes in the hospital."

"We asked him why he came back. He said, 'I wanted life. I missed you guys. I love you so much and I wanted to be with you.' He then put his arms around me and said, 'I was down there; it was black, Mom.' On questioning him, he recalled events which had happened before he was born, particularly of the time when my mother-in-law was in the hospital. There was no way he could have had any knowledge of these events. For a period of over a year he would continue with these tales and remarks. Today he recalls none of this."

This story makes me wonder about the memories young children retain, which disappear with age.

A spiritual progression takes us from lifetime to lifetime through many shifts of consciousness. With all the proof and evidence that can be presented, many people still refuse to believe in reincarnation due to their cultural traditions and doctrines. Evidence must be weighed by ourselves, for ourselves, using reason and intuition.

Thousands of cases of reincarnation have been studied by many important doctors and psychologists. People under hypnosis speak of mundane things in their time era such as what they are wearing, eating, the kind of work they do, and where they are living. Most of this information correlates with the historical facts of the era. Today a thinking person can believe in reincarnation on the basis of evidence. Yet people will believe in miracles and any unusual phenomena only as long as it happened thousands of years ago.

Death gives our spirit a rest and a chance to learn and evaluate what must be done in the next incarnation to complete our karma. We have to become aware of the meaning and progress of our life. Convictions of one's religion can be maintained without dogma. We must try to understand and tolerate various religious beliefs. They all say, "Love one another."

Bilocation of Spirits and Body

It is the 15th of March, 1980. The time is about 10:30 in the morning. The place is Mesa, Arizona.

Feeling a little tired I decide to lie down for a short nap. Suddenly I have a feeling like a quick "snap" to my body and I am no longer in it. I have no words to describe this transformation. There was no drowsiness or a "drifting off" feeling. It was instantaneous.

I am suddenly over a green forest in an altogether different part of the country. No more Arizona desert, but fairly heavy trees – pine and many others, a countryside similar to mid-Pennsylvania or upstate New York. I see a man who has just finished raping and strangling a young girl. A tree whose branches reach to the ground forms a sort of closed bower. The man is pushing her body under it and covering her with dead leaves and debris. She is a pretty girl, about 14 or 15 years old, whose face I shall never forget. Of dark complexion, brown eyes, and straight black hair, she wears a white middy blouse like a sailor top with blue trim and a navy blue pleated skirt. It appears to be the type of uniform a young girl would wear at a private institution or school.

In this transformation I am only a spectator. No physical contact or sound is possible. There is a bright sun overhead and it is a beautiful day.

The man I shall never forget. His image is burnt into my mind. He is about 5 foot, 7 or 8 inches tall, approximately 165 pounds, ruddy face with sandy reddish hair, slightly curly. He has a high forehead, a short beard with heavy sideburns terminating around his chin. He wears silver-rimmed eyeglasses. His disheveled white pants and jacket mark him as a kitchen or hospital worker. He moves to my right, over a mound or small hill. I am in a spiritual state, about 30 feet above him. A dirt, trail-like road leads out of this area to a secondary road. One side is cut through a small hill, about 15 feet high, composed of reddish dirt with black coal-like veins, like areas I have seen in my travels about Pennsylvania. Where it joined the road the trail was overgrown with bushes that had to be parted to exit.

I moved on, and not far in the distance I saw a school – a brick building with a large portico and tall white columns in front. Off to the side was a large grassy field area, similar to a playing court. People were milling about in front, starting a search for the missing girl. Three open trucks, like road-building dump trucks, arrived and the searchers climbed into them for a fruitless search. The murderer was one of them.

I had never seen the man nor the grounds I have been describing. Somehow, I had flashes of him working in a police barracks in that area as a cook or attendant of some sort.

"Click!" and I am wide awake again in my bed, but emotionally shaken. I take a pencil and note the high points of what I had seen. I try to draw a picture of the man, the girl, and the area.

What is it? What did it mean? Why did it happen to me?

Knowledgeable people in the psychic field later told me their theories, the main one being that a soul crying for help had made contact with me. The event could have happened then, in the past, or was going to occur in the future. I had no control.

Traveling has been my pleasure for many years. I know many of the areas of the United States well. Time after time, when I pass a building that even remotely resembles the one I saw during the time I was out of my body, my heart beats faster and the Adrenalin flows. Could this be the scene? My mind races until closer examination proves me wrong. I have driven on many secondary roads on a hunch or premonition when the land formation looked familiar. There is always the thought that around the next bend or turn, the scene will come into reality. I keep wondering if I am ever going to know the answer to this enigma. Will justice ever be done? Why me?

Chapter Eleven

OUT-OF-BODY EXPERIENCES AND MEMORY

OUT-OF-BODY EXPLANATIONS

Experiences of others can be easily dismissed as coincidence, fraud or error, but when it happens to you personally, your complacency is shaken. An out-of-body experience is very dramatic and results in a tremendous uncertainty that there is a bilocation of consciousness. The percipient retains full self-consciousness while actually viewing his physical body.

Those who have had a near-death experience seem to have the following in common:

> 1) A reduced fear of death.
> 2) A sense of invulnerability.
> 3) A feeling of special importance or destiny.
> 4) A belief in the special favor of God.
> 5) A belief in a continued existence.

Their consciousness has been flooded with a spiritual illumination. Researchers have attempted to explain these occurrences. The following theories have been advanced as explanation:

1) Independent soul. No need to explain further, it is just what it seems to be.
2) Hallucination. This is extra-sensory perception working on a non-conscious level (the subconscious), wherein it displays a hallucinatory scene to the conscious mind.
3) Mentally manipulatable state. There is a second body, real but non-physical, which is manipulated by conscious and non-conscious thought.
4) Altered states of consciousness. The brain or mind is programmed with commonplace assumptions that makes it take the particular form it does.
5) Interaction. Basic ESP exists, unexplainable with our current knowledge. The area we call mind is left out. We suspect this is some kind of energy existing independent of physical matter.

Some believe that the mind is accessible to science only in a materialistic way. They will not accept anything that cannot be verified by modern science. They attempt to explain consciousness in only physical terms. Disbelievers in life-after-death give four possible explanations:

1) Chemical – caused by drug administration.
2) Neurological – brain malfunctions near death, causing hallucinations.
3) Physiological – visions due to lack of oxygen or loss of blood sugar.
4) Psychological – possible sensory loss as death approaches.

But scientific investigation alone cannot explain the mysteries of near-death experiences. We have to deal in a spiritual realm to interpret. Death is a beginning, not an ending. Most people fear the word and the thought of dying. Yet they go to sleep daily and do not fear slipping into unconsciousness.

We know of the nerve connections between the brain and the body. Emotions create physical changes. Fear causes the heart to beat faster, anger raises blood pressure. We cry, we laugh, we become sexually stimulated through imagination. Meditation can control these symptoms. Swamis and yogis have controlled these tendencies to unbelievable degrees. Visualization techniques are now being studied for use in healing, called autogenic therapy.

Memory

What is memory? Why do we remember? How do we remember? Memory is as mysterious as consciousness. A prevalent theory is that it is not a function of the brain, but of consciousness. It is unexplainable in terms of brain substance and physics.

One scientific theory of memory is called "the brain theory." This regards memory as strictly a physiological process. Most of those who are opposed to any esoteric thinking follow this line of thought. It is rather technical and complex, but they call memory a "cerebral vibration." No one really knows the nature of the relationship between consciousness and the brain. Many theories are propounded.

Memory is never lost; it sinks into the subconscious and can be brought forth in many ways. Hypnotism, drugs, immanence of death, and yoga practices are some of the ways in which memory content can be returned.

During a hypnotic trance, memory becomes unbelievably vivid and retentive. Complete recall of forgotten events is common. Under hypnosis a subject can be made to see non-physical things and can also be made to black out their vision entirely.

If memory, like thought, is the motion of brain substance, how do we explain the total preservation of memory under hypnosis, when memory is a non-physical function of consciousness?

The world is fluid, ever-changing, totally interrelated. The cosmos is alive, organic, spiritual and material at the same time. The universe cannot be totally accounted for by conventional physics. We cannot leave out consciousness.

Psychic phenomena contradict the prevailing scientific views. They defy all laws of space and time. Reports are often undependable, as very little is reported under laboratory conditions. Many investigators feel that psychic manifestations are physical – electromagnetic fields, energy waves, radiations, emanations – all fields of force recognized by physicists.

At the opposite pole are the mystics and philosophers who claim that everything we see is illusion, the invisible is reality. Do psychic phenomena really exist or are they merely an extension of human abilities?

False Imagery

Two women, good friends and neighbors for many years, came to me with the following story, knowing of my interest in PSI phenomena.

They often play cards with a lady in their neighborhood whose home they think is haunted. Every night strange creaking noises emanate from the walls. Even stranger, when you stand in the hall at night and look at the sky through the bathroom window, a fiery cross appears.

I asked if they could get permission for me to see and hear this phenomena. The first thing that came to my mind was that in this area are many Indian graveyards and that perhaps this house was built over one.

On close examination I found that the sounds and crackling noises were caused by temperature change. When the house cooled down at night there was a natural contraction of the beams and joints, which created the sound effects. The fiery cross was caused by the bathroom window refracting an outside street light at a certain angle.

The window glass was defective and created an astigmatic effect when viewed from a certain angle. A fiery cross did seem to appear in the sky.

Rumors and stories can grow rampant when there is no prudent investigation. Many times there is a logical explanation for strange phenomena.

We should try to explain manifestations in physical terms (if possible) consistent with philosophic materialism. One of the best explanations for much of the strange phenomena that occur many times to humans is that there is a non-physical element existing in man. Call it the soul, or electro-chemical force, or whatever you wish. It is there.

Holography

Recent discoveries by neurophysiologists, neuropsychologists, neurobiologists and holographers indicate that the brain works holographically. Nerve impulses travel as waves of energy through as many as 100,000 neurons per second in three-dimensional nerve networks which are capable of storing 10 billion bits of information per cubic centimeter. Holography is the only known process that can pack information that tightly.

Removal of large amounts of brain tissues interferes very little with many functions, indicating that the entire brain is an overall wave field, or that a mentally imaged hologram is present.

The theory is that inside every person is a psychic hologram containing a staggering amount of information: the "picture" of the whole universe, or consciousness.

Some scientists think that since each cell contains information about the entire structure, making cloning possible, each cell in the brain holographically contains the whole consciousness. Present events are manifestations of infinite events contained in the holographic structure of the universe that knows no time or space.

Survival Research

Many scientists will not get involved in survival research. They seem to feel that while post-death survival may be a fact, it is not a fact that can be proved according to their present views of scientific criteria. How can we prove that human personality survives physical death, and how can we know the reality of that survival until we die? The difference of opinions is amazing.

In the Journal of the American Medical Association (Vol. 242, 11/23/79) is an article by a member of the faculty of Tufts University School of Medicine, who unequivocally states that there is no such thing as a valid after-death experience such as many of us have experienced and reported. In his view it is merely a hypoxic state during which we were dealing psychologically with anxieties regarding death.

About six months earlier, in the same journal (Vol. 242, 7/20/79), is a completely contrary view by two doctors who have researched and studied for years, and are considered to be knowledgeable scientists in this field. Two opposing views in the same journal. If you had read only one article and not the other, how would it affect your views on this subject?

Death makes it possible to understand the power of thought on another plane of existence. Death liberates us from all physical needs. Thought is a form of energy, strong enough to control energy in matter, which is done on another plane of existence.

The ultimate destiny for all is to return to a state of bliss and unity with God.

Documented out-of-body experiences by prudent scientific investigators prove that consciousness does exist separate from the physical body. I have only skimmed the surface of a complex subject with many fields, each one intertwined with the other and each one a science in itself. In a supernatural realm, human words and concepts are ineffable and inadequate in expressing feelings and experiences.

The mind of man now stands at the threshold of spiritual advancement. Ahead lies a major explosion of knowledge. New interpretations and discoveries that will dazzle the mind are coming. There is so much exploratory research yet to be done. Will the time ever come on Earth when we will all live in harmony? Amor vincit omnia (love conquers all).

Chapter Twelve

DEATH IS THE GATE OF LIFE

I am not a scientist or scholar but merely a seeker of truth. A few years ago I could have cared less, as I was embroiled in daily living. A massive coronary brought on a deep near-death experience and I went through the whole scene as described previously.

I then realized that you and I have a terminal illness, "life," which is always fatal.

What is death besides an end to life? The more scientific treatises and books that I read, the more I questioned the experts in this field. Since Moody popularized his research, a plethora of books and articles have been written.

A scientist as a scientist has to ignore that which does not adhere to any known physical laws, anything that cannot be brought about by scientific means and violates the laws of nature. I believe there are exceptions to this rule, whether we call the results metaphysical or miraculous. Too many people have experienced that which cannot be – yet is so.

The realization of the immanence of death makes us appreciate life. Looking backwards makes a great difference. I was once young, but were you ever old? Is my present your unknown future?

The wearing out of the physical body, a process called aging, makes it easier for us to abandon our mortal body when it is time for our spirit to leave. Suffering, pain and general dehabilitation help mold our mental state, making it easier to die.

We live in a collective culture; in death we are completely alone. Perhaps one of the fears of death is being alone. Many people avoid thinking about death because they have no true answers. Technology has brought us a long way, with many diversified opinions. Where does science stop and philosophy begin? A few scientific thinkers push knowledge forward.

In the course of life, death is a natural incident, coming to us all. It should not be dreaded, as it is simply a necessary step in our evolution. Let us wipe away the child-like gloom and terror that frightens us and realize that it is a beautiful, golden experience that leads us into a higher life.

Religious leaders take it for granted that God favors those that believe in Him. Yet why is it that many people who believe in God are skeptical of an after-life? Without strong scientific evidence, they feel it is improbable. Remember that while there is no scientific evidence that one does survive, there is also no evidence that one does not survive. The intense desire for immortality can warp a person's judgement in this area.

There is a great deal of investigation and literature on life after death; until you study and find your own answers, do not scoff at those who have had psychic experiences and want to enrich your life by sharing. The average mind finds it difficult to understand that which cannot be seen physically. We cannot see the air that surrounds us, we cannot see bacteria on which our lives depend, yet we know they are all around us. Our physical senses are like small windows which let in only a small amount of light. The spiritual world is another window enlarging our knowledge. Many ideas, while they cannot be scientifically proven, are worthy of consideration.

Esoteric seers who claim supernatural knowledge relate similar stories between them.

Fredrick Myers, a professor at Cambridge University, deceased (1901), a rigid scientific researcher, a contemporary of Einstein and Freud, was convinced by the evidence he collected, of existence after death. For twenty years after his death he allegedly communicated with different mediums and clairvoyants and told of various states of progression that the soul experiences on the so-called other side.

Emanuel Swedenborg wrote over 282 theological books during the 1700's, his most popular being *Heaven and Hell*. The Church of the New Jerusalem proselytizes on his teachings and has many parishioners around the world. He treats his heavenly experiences as though he were on another planet similar to earth. Were these hypnogogic delusions or visions? He tells of mysterious spheres of existence but is more Biblical than scientific, with many earthly details that are hard to believe.

In his "City of God," St. Augustine (354-430) pictures the progression of the soul throughout its various stages towards heaven.

Charles Leadbeater (1847-1934), a seer and occultist, a leader of the Theosophical school and voluminous author, relates very similar experiences.

The ancient Hebrew Kabala speaks of the many planes of progression before the soul's ultimate assimilation.

Are these all coincidental? The publicity that opened up and showed the similarity in near-death experiences may be the kind of next step necessary to bring out into the open people who have gone beyond our present range of vision, into these upper spheres, and beyond the simple near-death scenario. Let them relate what they have experienced. Let's wipe away the skepticism and awe and try to truly evaluate the mystic and clairvoyant. Is scientific proof always necessary to sustain a belief? Do you believe in God? Can you prove Him?

Although the following theories are philosophical rather than scientific, they appeal to me more than other literature I have read.

Those that have progressed beyond report that the astral planes are similar in certain respects to our present physical plane. Earthly matter has certain conditions. For example, it can be solid, liquid, or gaseous. The astral plane has different conditions of matter or astral density which correspond to the physical plane. You can still see physical aspects such as a house, walls, people, that you are accustomed to, but the particles composing the matter are visible in rapid motion, allowing the passage of wavelengths such as sight to pass through. All pain and fatigue disappear, but communication with the physical plane is not possible. Cognizance is only "one way" in this stage. Thoughts on the astral plane turn upward and physical matters denigrate as advancement begins. Life becomes more and more a life in a world of thought.

A person who has had low material desires on the physical plane will gradually lose these desires on the astral plane, before his next incarnation. The soul has been taught a lesson.

Man is free after death. No need to toil for food, clothing or lodging. Time is devoted to the realization of great delights of beauty, music and art. The comprehension of sciences are at his disposal. There's wonderful delight and no fatigue.

Those whose joy in life was in service to their fellow man find that their philanthropy will be used vigorously in helping both multitudes and individuals.

We are put on this earth for a purpose. Lessons must be learned that can be learned only here before advancement can occur. We will meet and recognize those with whom we have had an earthly bond of love. We may have to wait until we reach the plane they are on, but reunion is assured where affection exists. Love is a powerful bond on earth and in heaven.

We have a strong mental image of people we love that we take into the heavenly world with us. Their souls exist in the thought form we have of them and respond to that love in the future existence.

Heaven is a radiant reality, not a place, but a state of consciousness. It is indescribable using human words. It is a state of bliss obtainable only after death. I like to say it is ineffable. It is beyond comprehension of our present senses. How do you describe a rainbow to a blind person?

The soul that is not ready for the higher levels is returned for reincarnation. Its qualities are intensified by reiteration, experiences and information gained. As time goes on its heavenly life becomes longer and its bodily returns become shorter in number. The main lesson is to learn the glory of sacrifice – the devoting of your life in helping the human race. This is what all the great prophets and teachers such as Christ and Buddha have tried to tell us.

As the body needs daily sleep, the soul needs intermittent heavenly repose to attain the qualities necessary before Nirvana or final absorption into the Supreme Being can take place.

Hells are not at all like what we have been told or pictured, but are almost unexplainable. I have seen and felt the tremendous anguish and mental torment of rejected souls or spirits. When I went through my own death experience, I perceived during my travel through space and time towards the "light," a long column of grey, torpedo-like spirits going off into the distance. They appeared to be hooded, but where the face and shoulders should have been was a darkness except for a fiery red, similar to eyes. Tremendous woe emanated from them. There was a feeling of terrible mental pain as they moved on towards infinity.

Karma is a Hindu word meaning "accumulated destiny." It determines the nature of each incarnation. It is a sort of cause and effect law, existing beyond time and space. Some think that it ties in with the Akashic records, which are said to contain the life records of everyone, past, present and future. Some seers have been able to pipe into these records with tremendous psychic results.

Karmic law evaluates on merit everything a person does in his lifetime and relates it to the great scheme of the universe. Our impact on other individuals is most important. Actions and thoughts on all elements are taken into consideration from a God-like view. Every action and thought becomes part of our karma. Time is not an important factor. A deed done in a second can be as important as a lifetime of actions.

From studying these various views, I have formulated a personal theory (or call it a strong belief) that strengthens my conviction that death is not an end, but a beginning. The knowledge has been with us for centuries, but man has often disregarded the signs. I feel grateful to have been given a convincing sign.

Chapter Thirteen

THOUGHTS ON RELIGION

The Bible dominates and has become a way of life for many people. With a little imagination and a lot of faith these people foresee and foretell the past, present and future. Why is it that something that does so much good also creates so much harm with different interpretations by different faiths? I found that I personally could not relate to the Bible.

Why does a religious person have to embrace a certain religion? Most of us who have approached God cannot accept any one religion exclusively.

Most philosophy of religions is restricted to theological questions – such as the proof of God's existence. Isn't this the promise of most religions? I believe that most all religions are the same as far as God is concerned. He is above all mundane emotions.

"Do unto others as you would have them do unto you." This seems to be the cornerstone of all religious teachings. All the great religious teachers use (or used) these same words.

The average person is not knowledgeable about the many great religions of the world. Most of us are what we are because of our birth, or inheritance. We have no desire to change; we are content in our narrow cocoon.

As I studied, I wondered, with no printing presses in the ancient days, how much distortion was there in word-of-mouth passing of tales over the ages? How many times has the Bible been changed to fit the needs of the current political situations over the years? By whom? Certainly not God.

I felt that I could live an honest, ethical life, respect my fellow man, be responsible for my actions, and have my own rapport with God, without any formalized religion.

Talking to strongly religious people such as ministers or even scientific researchers who are in the field of near-death experiences, I have been surprised at how they attempt to fit NDE's into their religion – and not vice versa. The experience is above any specific religion. Practically everyone who has had an NDE becomes very cognizant of God and all ecclesiastical beauty. Most feel it difficult to conform to any formalized form of worship. They change to beings of love.

When you magnetize a bar of iron via an electric coil, some of the magnetism stays after the electric current is shut off. So it seems to be after this experience. There is a brilliancy of love which lowers in intensity with the passing of time. It becomes very difficult to pass this universal love on and still conform to the social standards we had previously.

How to relate and pass on this love is not easy, as most people feel that this is a "way out" topic. What can I give you to replace your earthly senses when I ask you to discard them? Again, I say there are no earthly terms to explain this experience. Can you see without eyes, or hear without ears? This is what happens when you leave your physical body.

What cosmic mode of action creates a being from a non-being? The beauty and thoughts in many Eastern religions can stir your soul. Your mind reaches out to create a harmony with the universe and empathy with all creation.

A spiritual person does not have to embrace a specific religion. God is within and all about us. The beauty of nature endlessly chants His divine presence. Nature and divinity are correlated. The stars, the sands of the sea, the wild flowers, the blades of grass, the silver bark of trees, the wings of birds and insects, lightning, the wind, clouds, the rippling waters, the perfume of flowers, the majestic sunsets, these and many other such things all heed His glory.

Our social, political and economic lives have become intertwined with religion. Religion as a body of belief should not be immune from criticism. Seek the truth that fits you.

Barriers of selfishness and blindness divide human hearts and keep us apart. Let us stop confusing that which is, with that which we imagine. Once our minds are cognizant of God's love, there is no room for hatred. Most evil is caused by ignorance. Humanity begins when we ask, "Where am I from? Where am I going? Why am I here?" Religion without philosophy is sentiment or fanaticism. While philosophy without religion is mental speculation.

Religion is primarily a human thing and should be concerned with human improvement – individually and socially. Buddha, Confucius and Lao Tzu taught non-theistic religions. Millions of people are outside of any church or formalized religion. How can we infer what these people are when judging by a Christian religion? Or any other? All humans must realize that they alone are responsible for the world of their dreams and they alone have the power for its achievement.

As knowing science helps cure our physical ills, knowing God can cure us of hatred, anger and selfishness. Deep understanding creates peace and brotherhood. We are limited in our earthly knowledge and have many disappointments, but in the blinding divine light that permeates our senses in the presence of God, we know of true love and the joy of immortality.

God directs all material nature; all beauty and wonderful things work under His direction. The position of God is that of supreme consciousness.

We love ourselves and consider our way as the only correct way; we reject anything strange. Even though some men and customs are strange to us, we are all children of God and must respect other people and their ways.

Our senses are very inadequate for comprehending the unnatural or invisible. We cannot see in the infra-red or ultra-violet spectrums or that which lies beyond, yet we know they exist. Neither can we see the world beyond our physical senses. We have a spirit or soul, something different from our physical earth body, within us. Most people are interested only in satisfying their carnal appetites. Eating, sleeping and mating are far more important than seeking a transcendental knowledge, or understanding themselves.

To relate to an entity of pure love and knowledge that has no describable physical form but projects as a blinding, searing light, is almost incomprehensible. Maybe this is why mankind worships an intermediary in a human form that he can feel more comfortable with – God's prophets – who are on a more humanoid level and can intercede for him. What if we were not born into a religion but gave equal time to the study of all religions and then decided on that which we felt most comfortable? How much greater our degree of tolerance would be.

Where did the tremendous knowledge of the ancient prophets and seers come from? Most of their religious laws were health and social laws so that people could exist together in harmony. An uneducated populace could not comprehend some other reasoning for these laws, so they were told that "God says," and blindly obeyed out of fear.

Everything that lives must die: men, animals, plants, germs. Only man knows this.

Death should be faced fearlessly and sensibly, as a friend, not as something to be feared.

According to modern medicine, the actual time of physical death has changed. A short time ago it was when the heart and respiration stopped; now it is when the brain current stops.

Science does not know exactly when death occurs. Respiration may stop, the heart may stop, brain waves may stop, but the individual cells may be alive for a while. Death occurs when the soul leaves the body; but how do we explain those who return from a near-death experience, making this a contradictory statement?

Is chemistry the answer to determining the time of death? There are three types of death: 1) Organic. 2) Cellular. 3) Spiritual.

From the dawn of history man has been seeking immortality. It is not within our physical grasp. It is not to be found on earth but in a different place, in a different time, in a different form.

Do we really know what has happened when a person who is clinically dead returns? Could there be a space-time continuum, with the time almost stopping? (Einstein's Gamma Effect). Can any doctor tell you when life really begins? Time is the abundance of what we are able to experience, it's not a specific hour or date. Your physical life and your environment are related somewhat like your soul and body.

Due to the shortness of our time on earth, we should live fully. Smell the roses, appreciate the beauty of the world.

Our attitude towards death will make it much easier for our souls to leave when our time comes, and may even lessen our physical pain. An empty, unfulfilled life can cause despair at termination, while a full, satisfying life makes the transition easier.

Though there is no actual proof, most theologians and scientists believe that the soul is infused into the body by a divine being and that it can exist apart and continue after physical termination of the body. Death is only a rebirth into the cosmos from which we originated. One of the main purposes of life is to live and experience. The acquisition of knowledge is of the utmost importance. All our parapsychological and theological knowledge confirm that death is not the end but merely a transformation into another existence.

Religion originally helped mankind to live together in harmony. Today it causes a great amount of polarization. Religions teach religion more than spirituality. Religions are basically on the right track. Each individual is co-creator with God and controller of his own destiny. We should remember that we are part of God and have a certain divinity which we must respect, and act accordingly. In early times, laws and beliefs were not passed on in any written form so misunderstandings were common. The Bible's context was changed more and more to human viewpoints, for the purpose of keeping in power those who held the reins at that time. Man decided what was allowed to be true. Vested interests of religious teachers affected the teachings of the times.

This created inconsistencies in religion which made thinking people doubt parts of the faith that was taught them. Man today, being more educated, finds it difficult to accept some of the child-like tenets of the Bible.

Religion as a body of belief should be open to criticism. Confrontation with scientific principles may cause some erosion. Most people have inherited their religion the same as the color of their skin or eyes and feel uncomfortable when controversial questions are brought up that are inconsistent with what they have been taught. Could the fear of death be the reason they accept almost any tenet?

It is best that we seek the truth that fits us, and boldly strip away any philosophical and intellectual dogmas that are well-meaning but not necessarily true, used by people who attempt to influence our mental attitudes.

In the body are hands, legs and various parts. Most parts are engaged in satisfying the stomach and cooperating with it. Fingers cannot enjoy food; they must give it to the stomach to receive the benefit of it. You must give service to God to receive the benefits of God.

Every cell in our body is independent, yet part of the tissue which is part of the organ which is part of the body. Independent man is also part of a race, which is part of all mankind. We are all part of a greater order sent here for "God's purpose," to Whom we must return to become part of the whole. The soul and God are eternal. To understand God, we must first know ourselves.

Intellectual cleverness does not permit us to be ignorant of our spiritual nature. We cannot be physically alive and spiritually dead. The material world is a reflection of the spiritual world. It is like a shadow that has no substance, yet we know from the shadow that there has to be something to create the shadow.

The hope of immortality gives people strength in this life. Without the promise of life beyond the grave, there would be a great deal more despair. To endure the present, dream of the future. To obtain enlightenment, struggle for knowledge, light and guidance.

Belief in life after death dates back to our earliest beginnings. Early man knew that there was more to life than the physical senses he experienced. This world is a "training ground" for our ultimate destination. A spirit is an intelligence in another dimension. The similarity of the experiences of those who were clinically dead and revived is proof of life after death.

The spirit body is a replica of our physical body. It contains all our thoughts (conscious or unconscious), desires, knowledge, and character. Death frees us from our physical bodies. We will be well and happy in beautiful surroundings with loved ones and friends who have made the transition before us.

The spirit body or soul is perfect. There are no material needs. There is no such thing as time or distance as we know it. Our thoughts are where and what we are.

We have become so involved with our material life that we forget that it is not our true life. Our time here is so short compared to the eons to come. Our true life starts with our transition at death and begins with what we have made of ourselves on a mortal level. Our rush for gold has blunted our seeking of understanding fellow humans. Complacency is prevalent. The millennium can come only when we share a unity of ideas and all knowledge, thereby attaining a peaceful coexistence. Liberation from physical needs comes later, and is one of the great benefits of death. The best is yet to come, including a realization of immortality.

Immortality is defined from various viewpoints:

Biologically: We are immortal if we have children.
Socially: We are immortal as long as others think of us.
Morally: We are immortal if we have contributed something good to life while we lived.
Life's Cycle: Makes us immortal if we remember the basic laws of physics – nothing can be created or destroyed, but only transformed.

Death is a basic function and a universal event. Most all of us have an anxiety about non-existence and a fear or agony about the transition. What a beautiful awakening we have coming! Do not demand a scientific proof, as there is no science or philosophy that can match up with your present mental connection to the after-life and immortality. Without vision we perish.

A Butterfly
by G. Eustace Owen

A butterfly rested upon a flower,
  Gay was he and light as a flake.
And there he met a caterpillar
  Sobbing as though his heart would break;
It hurt the happy butterfly
  To see a caterpillar cry.

Said he, "Whatever is the matter?"
  And may I help in any way?"
"I've lost my brother," wept the other,
  "He's been unwell for many a day;
Now I discover, sad to tell,
  He's only a dead and empty shell."

"Unhappy grub, be done with weeping,
  Your sickly brother is not dead;
His body's stronger and no longer
  Crawls like a worm, but flies instead.
He dances through the sunny hours
  And drinks sweet nectar from the flowers."

"Away, away deceitful villain.
  Go to the winds where you belong.
I won't be grieving at your leaving,
  So take away your lying tongue.
Am I a foolish slug or snail,
  To swallow such a fairy tale?"

"I'll prove my words, you unbeliever.
  Now listen well, and look at me.
I am none other than your brother,
  Alive and well and fancy free.
Soon you'll be with me in the skies
  Among the flirting butterflies."

"Ah!" cried the mournful caterpillar.
  "'Tis clear I must be seeing things.
You're only a spectre sipping nectar,
  Flicking your ornamental wings,
And talking nonsense by the yard.
  I will not hear another word."

The butterfly gave up the struggle.
  "I have," he said, "no more to say."
He spread his splendid wings and ascended
  Into the air and flew away.
And while he fluttered far and wide,
  The caterpillar sat and cried.

Chapter Fourteen

RAISON D'ETRE

Years have now passed since my near-death experience, years of searching and wondering, "Why me?" Stunned at first, I was quiet and reticent, afraid to talk for fear of being different. Then, with love bursting its bonds, my odyssey started. All through my delving and questioning the primary thought was, "Why me?" The answer is now partly clear.

My youngest daughter and I have been very close in our ability to discuss and comprehend psychic experiences. About a year after my NDE she told me about a psychic medium whom she thought I should see. I, being of scientific mind, "pooh-poohed" this idea. My mistaken thought was that this would be like a fortune telling experience – the dim room, crystal ball, the usual generalities that one can interpret to mean most anything.

Out of curiousity, I decided to go. I was stunned by the experience. It was a bright, sunny afternoon. My wife, daughter and I made the trip together. My daughter took notes and recorded the conversation.

We met the psychic, a rather pleasant elderly lady who was visiting here from New Zealand. After a few moments of generalities, she said a small prayer and then began to talk. There was no hocus-pocus or dimming of lights. I was amazed that she had an intimate knowledge of my family and wife. Even if she were a mental telepath, there was no way she could have gained this knowledge. I resided in Massachusetts, she came from New Zealand, and we met in Arizona.

I was given information of which I had no prior knowledge and later found to be true. When I asked why I was being allowed a second chance at life, I was told that one of the reasons was that I was here "to teach the children." This had no meaning for me at that time. This was long before I had any idea that I would lecture or write on my experiences, which up to this time I considered very personal.

About a year later I was prevailed upon by a young friend of mine, a high school teacher, to talk to his class about my experience. They were doing an ESP study. I had never spoken in public but, with much trepidation, I finally agreed. When I was introduced to the audience, a transformation came over me. Without any notes or preparation, my message just flowed out of me. Other teachers came to see me and asked if I would speak to their classes. What started as a small symposium became an all day affair. When I heard the tapes played back, I was pleasantly surprised – I couldn't believe I was so coherent and convincing.

One day much later when I was reading over the notes on the psychic reading, I suddenly realized what the phrase "to teach the children" meant. After this I found I was able to lecture and relate my NDE and post-death studies to any group anywhere. I have spoken at symposiums, colleges, on radio and television and have been able to help dispel the fear of death for many people.

However, I believe the greatest purpose God had for my return was the care of my wife, Natalie.

After my heart attack, the doctors found so many things wrong with my health that I knew my time was limited. Worry about leaving my wife, who had been dependent on me all her married life, was my first priority. I found a lovely trailer village in Arizona where a large group of very supportive people live. This, I thought, would be a great place for a woman alone. However, man proposes and God disposes.

After a routine medical check and biopsy, her doctor told us that she had advanced cancer, with maybe six months left. With good supportive oncology, this was extended to three years. My wife had been a doubter of existence after physical death. She had, after listening to me, gained faith in the immortality of the soul previous to this doomsday news. This I was thankful for; it helped sustain her.

As she slowly declined, I was able to take care of her – changing dresses, give injections, cooking and cleaning and doing the multitude of things necessary to sustain life. I truly believe that this was part of God's purpose in allowing my return.

Now I wish to tell of a most wonderful thing that Natalie experienced. We have a new grandson in California who was about 18 months old when Natalie made the transition we call death. The previous summer when he was nine months old was the last time she spent with him. She wanted so dearly to see him again. I kept saying that as soon as she felt a little better we would go, maybe next week, and so on.

Natalie died at 4:30 P.M. at the Mesa Lutheran Hospital in Arizona on July 25, 1984. At about 4:45 P.M. I phoned to notify my son and his wife, who live in the San Diego area of California. The baby was at a baby sitter's house; my daughter-in-law was at work. She went to pick him up about an hour later. A few days later she told me this story:

"When I went to get the child, the baby sitter told me that at about 4:30 P.M. she was playing with the child. He suddenly withdrew, went to the side of the room, looked up for a few moments and said, 'Bye-bye, Grandma.' When I told the baby sitter that my mother-in-law had passed on at this exact time, we both had chills and goose-bumps."

After this, how can anyone not believe in the immortality of the soul? Natalie made the trip.

Death of a loved one brings mixed emotions. You don't want them to leave and yet you pray for them to go swiftly when the suffering overwhelms you. The despair is soul rending at first. The presence of family and friends helps alleviate the heart-tearing anguish. Yet when you are alone and the enormity of the entire scene hits you, there is no solace. You know that only the body is dead and that your loved one is at peace and in an eternal love. Yet the loss of a shared life strikes you hard.

Time goes by, you live and somehow get through your daily tasks. The sorrow starts receding. Some friend comes by and innocently asks, "How is your wife?" The wound rips open again, but the hurt is shorter. You cope with the mundane daily tasks that you gave no thought to previously, as this was your spouses domain. It is not the same, but you exist.

In a way you are glad that the loved one went first as you would not want her to go through this period. It is easier to die. The spiritual life is far better than the physical. You know this, and yet you find yourself occasionally talking to her absence and ranting against the fate that deprived you of the few more years you might have shared. You feel guilty when you do something you know she would also enjoy very much. Life goes on, one day at a time.

I believe that death is a natural incident that is coming to all of us. I have no dread or fear, as I feel that it is simply a natural step in my evolution. I am here for a purpose. A lesson must be learned before advancement. Reunion on another plane with those I loved on this earthly plane is assured. Love is a powerful bond on earth and in heaven. My personal realm of experiential knowledge is my own life situation. Life is experience.

EPILOGUE

My odyssey to find the secret of life beyond physical existence has taken many paths. The truth is so elusive. When I recently enrolled in a course in philosophy and religion, I was amazed at the intolerance of the professors to other viewpoints. The average student seemed concerned only with pleasing the teacher, becoming attuned to his views, receiving a good mark.

It was then I realized that many speakers merely have to confront an audience to have their statements accepted. The audience feels that the orator would not be in the speaker's position if he did not know what he was talking about. This is not so.

How many times have you heard in advertising that this product contains something like "hexorinsorcinal 37 extra-strength?" So what? Does this add anything to the product that is to the good? Maybe it is *not* good for you. The average person never questions what he doesn't know for fear of showing ignorance, when he should be seeking knowledge.

Unfortunately, public opinion creates public consensus. That is why demagogues like Hitler were able to sway a whole nation. I urge that you question all facts and premises, especially when dealing with the paranormal. What makes it TRUE?

Perhaps if you had read or studied the same facts as I, you would come to a different conclusion. Why accept anything verbatim?

Although I grant that the field of parapsychology and the study of the world beyond has its charlatans and sensationalists (as do many other areas), I am convinced that the evidence of a life-beyond-life is massive, solid and believable. Why should I, a former doubter, have been given the chance to "see with new eyes?" I believe that part of my task is to share my knowledge and faith with you. If I have helped a few of you, my studies will have been worthwhile.

It is only the surface of life that we see. Behind its manifestations are deeper laws. When our souls are awakened by love, hatred cannot abide. Ignorance creates evil. As scientific knowledge creates a better physical world, so will the knowledge of God bring about universal peace and brotherhood.

Earthly knowledge is limited; it despairs over mysteries it cannot solve. When God and Love enter our hearts, mysteries cease.

Suggested Readings

Books that have affected my thinking. Some are full of knowledge and others merely add a few drops, but where else does one seek answers to unanswerable questions without drawing on the composite thoughts of others, rejecting and accepting ideas and understandings?

Due to the number of entries, only author and title are included.

* Denotes those that were most important to me.

Abell & Singer, *Science and the Paranormal.*
Allen, Bearne and Smith, *Energy, Matter and Forms.*
Atwater, P., *Coming Back to Life.*
*Banerjee, H.N., *Lives Unlimited: Reincarnation East and West.*
*Barnet, L., *The Universe and Dr. Einstein.*
Bartlett, L.E., *PSI Trek.*
Barber, J. (ed.), *Psychological Approaches to the Management of Pain.*
Bayless, R., *Experiences of a Psychical Researcher.*
Bhadragaka, *The Dhammapada.*
Bach, Richard, *Illusions.*
Boch, M., *Had You Been Born in Another Faith.*
Brain, L.J., *The Last Taboo.*
Bradley, D.R., *Psychic Phenomena.*
*Brienstein, Karl, *Beyond the Fourth Dimension.*
Cageau, E.J., and Scott, *Exploring the Unknown.*
*Calder, Nigel, *Einstein's Universe.*
Carminera, Gina, *Many Mansions.*
Carminera, Gina, *The World Within.*
Cayce, Hugh, *Venture Inward.*
Christopher, M., *Search for the Soul.*
*Christian, James, *Philosophy.*

Clarke, Farley and Welfare, *World of Strange Powers*.
Daniken, Eric von, *Miracle of the Gods*.
*Dethlefsen, Thorwald, *Voices from Other Lives*.
Doncee, J.E., *Philosophical Anthropology*.
Ebon, Martin (ed.), *The Psychic Reader*.
Ebon, Martin (ed.), *Beyond Space and Time*.
Ebon, Martin (ed.), *Psychic Warfare*.
Eisenbud, Jules, M.D., *Paranormal Foreknowledge*.
Evans, Hillary, *Visions and Apparitions*.
Ferris, A.R. (translator), *Spiritual Sayings of Kahil Gibran*.
Flammonde, Paris, *The Mystic Healer*.
Fiore, Edith, *The Unquiet Dead*.
Fodor, Nandor, *Between Two Worlds*.
*Ford, Arthur, *The Life Beyond Death*.
*Gallup, George Jr., *Adventures in Immortality*.
Geis, H. (Dick and William), *The New Soviet Psychic Discoveries*.
Goodman, Jeffrey, *We Are the Earthquake Generation*.
Goodman, Jeffrey, *Psychic Archeology*.
Goodwin, John, *Occult America*.
Head and Scranton, *Reincarnation in World Thought*.
Head and Scranton, *Reincarnation: The Phoenix Fire Mystery*.
Holzer, Hans, *Patterns of Destiny*.
Holzer, Hans, *Psychic Photography*.
Holzer, Hans, *Psychic Investigators*.
Holzer, Hans, *Psychic Research*.
Holzer, Hans, *Born Again*.
Huxley, Aldous, *Heaven and Hell*.
Huxley, Aldous, *The Dawn of Perception*.
*International Assoc. of Near Death Studies, *I.A.N.D.s Journal*.
Jacobson, N., M.D., *Life Without Death*.
*Knight, David, *The ESP Reader*.
Kreeft, Peter, *Love is Stronger than Death*.
Kreeft, Peter, *Philosophical Questions in Religion*.
Kaufman, Phillip, *The Wheel of Death*.
Klimo, Jan, *Channeling*.

Kolosimo, Peter, *Timeless Earth*.
Kasturi, M., *The Life of Bhagava Sri Sai Baba*.
Kreskin, *The Amazing World of Kreskin*.
Langone, John, *Death is a Noun*.
Leadbeater, C.W., *The Life After Death*.
Lewis, C., *The Problem of Pain*.
Lewis, C., *Miracles*.
Lundhal, Craig, *A Collection of Near Death Research Readings*.
McAdams, E., and Bayless, R., *The Case for Life After Death*.
*Mishlove, Jeffrey, *The Roots of Consciousness*.
Montgomery, Ruth, *Here and Hereafter*.
*Moody, Raymond, M.D., *Life After Life*.
*Moody, Raymond, M.D., *Reflections on Life After Life*.
*Moody, Raymond, M.D., *The Light Beyond*.
Mookerjee, Agitcoomar, *Kundalini: The Arousal of Inner Energy*.
Moore, Marcia, *Hypersentience*.
Moss, P., and Keeton, J., *Encounters With the Past*.
Moss, Thelma, *The Body Electric*.
Myers, F.W., *Human Personality and its Survival of Bodily Death*.
*Nash, C.B., *Parapsychology*.
*Ornstein, Robert, *The Mind Field*.
Osborne, Arthur, *The Meaning of Personal Existence*.
Overlee, V.W., *The Psychic*.
Pauwels and Bergier, *Impossible Possibilities*.
Prabhapada, Swami, *The Bhagavad-Gita*.
Prabhapada, Swami, *Coming Back*.
Prabhapada, Swami, *Life Comes From Life*.
Purcel, *Thinking About Religion*.
Randal, J., *Parapsychology and the Nature of Life*.
Randi, James, *Flim Flam*.
Reyers, Benito F., *Scientific Evidence of the Existence of the Soul*.
Richards, J.J., *Sorrat*.
*Ring, Kenneth, *Life at Death*.
*Ring, Kenneth, *From Here to Omega*.
Robinson, Dianne, *To Stretch a Plank*.

*Rogers, L.W., *Elementary Theosophy*.
Rogo, Scott, *Mind Beyond the Body*.
Rogo, Scott, *In Search of the Unknown*.
Rogo, Scott, *Minds in Motion*.
Rogo, Scott, *Psychic Breakthroughs Today*.
Samuels, M.N., *Seeing With the Mind's Eye*.
Sagan, Carl, *Cosmos*.
Schwartz, B., *Psychic Noxus*.
Shallus, Michael, *One Time*.
*Smart, N., *The Long Search*.
Smith, Suzy, *The Book of James*.
Smulligan, R., *5000 B.C. and Other Philosophical Fantasies*.
Spangler, David, *Revelation*.
Steiger, Brad, *You Will Live Again*.
*Stevenson, Ian, *Twenty Cases Suggestive of Reincarnation*.
Stromberg, Gustaf, *The Soul of the Universe*.
Stuart, R., *The Strange World of Frank Edwards*.
Stuart, L., *Life Forces*.
Tannous, Alex, *Alex Tannous*.
Taylor, C., *Superminds*.
Taylor, J., *Science and the Supernatural*.
Timms, Moira, *Prophecies and Predictions*.
Vanderman, George, *Psychic Roulette*.
*Walker, Benjamin, *Beyond the Body*.
Watkins, Wm. J., *The Psychic Experiment Book*.
Warshofsky, Fred, *Doomsday*.
*White, John, *Poleshift*.
Whitten, J., and Fish, J., *Life Between Life*.
Wilson, Colin, *Dark Dimensions*.
Wilson, Colin, *Mysteries*.
Wilson, Colin, *After Life*.
Wilson, Ian, *All in the Mind*.
*Wolman, Benjamin (ed.), *Handbook of Parapsychology*.
Zaleski, Carol, *World Journeys*.

About the Author

Robert Pinansky was a member of the International Association of Near Death Sudies and was a frequent lecturer on his experiences and philosophies. He has spoken at schools, colleges, to hospice workers, religious and medical groups, the general public and on the radio and television.

At the University of Connecticut, Psychology Department, his Near Death Experience was investigated and corroborated by Dr. Kenneth Ring. He has been interrogated and researched by Dr. Grayson of the University of Michigan Hospital, and Professor C. P. Flynn of the Department of Sociology and Anthropology of Miami University, plus other eminent researchers in this field throughout the world.

Mr. Pinansky was the author of several articles in this same field.

Triumph of the Human Spirit:
The Greatest Achievements of the Human Soul
and How Its Power can Change Your Life
by Paul Tice.

This book is about those who changed the entire course of history. They did not start with money, power, or great armies—all they had was an idea, and a passion for the truth. Gandhi, Joan of Arc, Dr. King and others died for their ideas but made the world a better place. This book outlines how an intuitive spiritual knowledge, or "gnosis," provided these people with guidance and helped to create the most incredible spiritual moments that the world has ever known. These events are all part of our spiritual evolution. We have learned from past mistakes, have become more tolerant toward others, and the people in this book have been signposts——pointing us collectively toward something greater. This book also shows how a spiritual triumph of your own can be achieved. Various exercises will strengthen the soul and reveal its hidden power. Unlike the past, in today's Western world we are free to explore the truth without fear of being tortured or executed. As a result, the rewards are great. This is the perfect book for all those who believe in spiritual freedom and have a passion for the truth.

BT-574 · ISBN 1-885395-57-4 · 295 pages
6 x 9 · trade paper · illustrated · $19.95

Call Toll Free:
888 909 7474
NEXUS Magazine 2940 E. Colfax #131, Denver, CO

- **GOVERNMENT COVER-UPS**
- **SUPPRESSED SCIENCE**
- **ALTERNATIVE HEALTH**
- **UFO'S & THE UNEXPLAINED**

ORDER YOUR FREE ISSUE!!

Pay the bill which follows to continue your subscription or keep the issue with no obligation

Zen and the Lady
by Claire Myers Owens

Now back in print! When this book was first published in 1979 it was praised by the most respected spiritual researchers and psychologists of the time including Ken Wilbur, Kenneth Ring, Charles Tart, Jack Kornfield and Willis Harmon. Her earlier work was also praised by Abraham Maslow and Aldous Huxley.

Zen and the Lady is the personal story of an American woman's journey into Zen, beginning in her 70th year and continuing into her eighties. In this book Claire Myers Owens brings the reader with her on the path to enlightenment. It is a journey of spiritual development, perfect for those seeking the same type of growth, no matter what background or tradition one is from. Claire is no longer alive today, but her powerful and touching story will live on in the hearts of those who read it. This book is already considered a classic of Western mystical literature.

"All struggles were ended, all seeking forgotten, all dualities abandoned. Every hope fulfilled. Every question answered. Every problem resolved—briefly, if not for all time. I was content..." —from *Zen and the Lady*

"A beautiful tale, artfully told... I've read a number of spiritual autobiographies, including several within a Zen setting, but ZEN AND THE LADY is without parallel." —Kenneth Ring

"I found it absolutely fascinating and a totally absorbing story, a superb blend of autobiographical remembrance and sophisticated psychological insights." —Ken Wilbur

"Thank you for being an inspiration to us all." —Willis Harmon

"It is a treasure trove... of wisdom." —Sonja Margulies
                    Journal of Transpersonal Psychology

"Beautiful." —Jack Kornfield

"Fascinating." —Charles Tart

ISBN 1-58509-129-4 • 192 pages • 6 x 9 • perfect bound • $17.95.

To order with credit card call **1-800-700-TREE (8733)**, or mail $22.45 to The Book Tree, PO Box 16476, San Diego, CA 92176 (CA residents add 7.75 % sales tax).

www.thebooktree.com

www.ingramcontent.com/pod-product-compliance
Lightning Source LLC
Chambersburg PA
CBHW031650040426
42453CB00006B/260